ONE by ONE

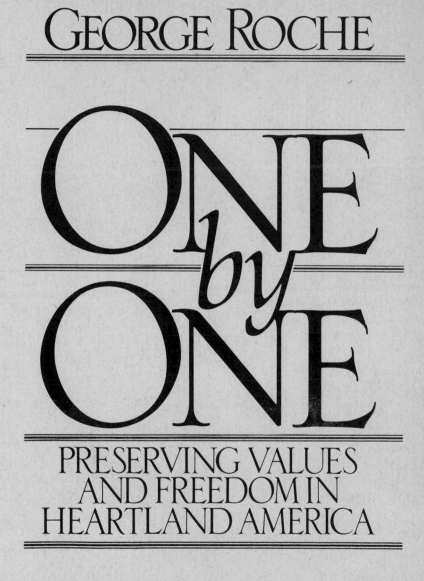

GEORGE ROCHE

ONE by ONE

PRESERVING VALUES AND FREEDOM IN HEARTLAND AMERICA

Books by the Hillsdale College Press include: volumes by George Roche, President of Hillsdale College; *Champions of Freedom* series on economics; *The Christian Vision* series; and other works.

ONE BY ONE: PRESERVING VALUES AND FREEDOM IN HEARTLAND AMERICA

First Printing 1990
Library of Congress Catalog Card Number: 90-083368
ISBN 0-916308-84-7

Cover design by Ben Santora
Printed and bound by Edwards Brothers, Ann Arbor, Michigan, with special thanks to Martin Edwards

To my family
and
some special friends

They know who they are . . . .

CONTENTS

viii   *Contents*

FOREWORD

With the fall of the Berlin Wall and the demise of institutionalized communism in Eastern Europe, we have witnessed the most astonishing miracle since the end of World War II. In a more subtle sense, the significance of this rejection of communism is even wider in scope than was the ending of the World War.

Yet we must not be lulled into a false sense of security on either the foreign or domestic fronts. The Castros, Gadhafis and Arafats are still present, loosing their damage or terrorism on the world; and in our own country many matters are getting worse. George Roche takes on these matters—with the courage and honesty to attack what is wrong; with the optimism and hope to offer constructive solutions and to count the blessings for what is right about America.

This book documents our troubles with the government, with institutional education, with political aberrations, with collective control, with immorality and with impiety. Dr. Roche asks that we return to the sanctity of the individual and to God. He believes that *ideas*—not money, not power, not bigness, not government, not laws—but ideas rule the world, and that we need to return to the good old ideas and to reject the new bad ones.

In this light, he says of President Reagan:

> Where President Reagan really did succeed was in changing the terms of the debate in this country.
>
> Mr. Reagan's prime achievement is that he spoke over the heads of the establishment, over the heads of both political parties, over the heads of

the media, over the heads of the bureaucracy, over all the intrigues and politicking and weird thinking that marks life inside the Beltway. And he did this all the time. He spoke to us, the forgotten folk out here in the country, who just happen to *be* the country. He spoke to us about our own concerns, our real concerns: about the status of our children's education, about our savings for our old age, the regulation of our farms and jobs and businesses, about what was happening in every aspect of our lives.

At Hillsdale one can mention "God" on campus without fear of reprisal from those exclaiming separation of church and state. And liberal arts there are precisely that—liberating, moving toward freedom.

The College's movement toward this freedom was heightened when the school engaged in a principled battle against then HEW, which was attempting to rein in the little heartland college and subject it to government control even though it had never been accused or found guilty of any improprieties. Goliath had determined David guilty until proven innocent.

As the title of this book suggests, human and humane progress is always made one by one, not many by many. It is the individual who achieves, not the group, and he or she does so one *by* one, that is, *with* others. The altruism here is in the form of voluntary cooperation, one individual unto another, as distinguished from coerced control by a group.

Realizing how humane progress is achieved, Hillsdale College, under the leadership of Dr. George Roche and its trustees, will steadfastly continue to refuse federal money and the control that accompanies that aid. Government grants and loans are not welcome, and students who win scholarships on merit or who need financial help will get the funds entirely from a volunteering private sector.

How wonderfully refreshing is this College's stand.

La Jolla, California   Frank Shakespeare
September 1990

A Hillsdale College trustee, Frank Shakespeare is the former U.S. Ambassador to the Vatican and former senior vice president of CBS.

THE HILLSDALE IDEA
Sesquicentennial: Hillsdale College, 1844–1994

"What hath God wrought?"

A strange new device translated these pious words into impulses over an electrical wire. Another device at a distance received them instantly. History had changed. The barriers of time and space had fallen. Direct and immediate communication would henceforth be practical between anyone, in any land.

The words of Samuel F. M. Morse, farsighted yet humble, were a worthy message for a new era. For twelve years he had toiled to perfect his invention. He called it a telegraph, from Greek roots meaning "long distance" and "writing."

The year was 1844.

Please note the date. We will want to understand some perspectives from that long-ago time. This is difficult. More than twice man's "three score years and ten," two lifetimes, have passed. Indeed, from the view of 1844, five lifetimes have passed: for the average life expectancy then was less than thirty years. The changes since have been dizzying.

In 1844, the Republic was young and robust. Within recent memory, two of its great Founders had died: Thomas Jefferson and John Adams, eerily, on the same day, July 4, 1826, the fiftieth anniversary of the Declaration of Independence. In little more than a half century, the population had grown about fourfold—from some 4,000,000 in 1790 to 17,069,453 in the 1840 census. The number of states had doubled, from the original thirteen to twenty-six. But in area, the country was only a quarter of the size it is today.

You would not recognize a map of America then. Its western reach extended no further than states along the Mississippi River: Louisiana, Arkansas and Missouri to the south, Illinois to the north. In part of Illinois, the Mississippi was the western frontier. Twenty-four of our present states were yet to join the union: Florida in the south and all of the states to the west and north including the Great Plains, Hawaii and Alaska (the last two well over a century later). Only a few adventurers and trappers had penetrated the far west. The discovery of gold in California and the great westward migration it spurred still lay ahead.

Few of the great inventions we take for granted existed in 1844. The telephone was thirty years in the future, electric power forty, radio and the automobile fifty, the airplane sixty. Television, transistors, jet aircraft and computers were all a century away. Almost all transport was horse-drawn. The only powered conveyances were steamboats and the steam locomotive (introduced less than fifteen years earlier). Plumbing, where it existed, was crude, glass windows were a luxury, and household appliances as we know them did not exist. From our perspective, perhaps—but not from theirs—life, for most, was laborious, and amenities few. We would, however, be greatly mistaken in thinking our own life richer or more fulfilling.

It was a time of great optimism, invention and energy, and of deep conviction in the "Great Experiment" that was America. Our country was secure in her faith, echoing St. Paul's famous declaration, "Where the spirit of the Lord is, there is liberty." It was not sodden, as it is now, with "problems" and guilt and self-doubts. America, born in a pilgrimage of unbelievable hardship from the Old World, was to be the "City on the Hill." A church was one of the first buildings at every crossroads settlement. The future looked grand.

In the realm of politics America's watchword was liberty for all. Such phrases as "the land of the free" were by no means the exhausted political slogans they became later. They were the beacon and the reality.

Do I exaggerate? You judge. In 1844, the spirit of the Revolution still animated America. Government was the implacable enemy of liberty, a potential tyrant, a barely necessary evil to be treated with suspicion and eternal vigilance and bound by the chains of the Constitution. Man was by nature free.

Accordingly, the power and reach of the federal government were duly and strictly limited. People usually lived their whole lives without encountering any federal presence other than the postman. And even the Post Office was under furious assault at the time from private entrepreneurs who did the job faster and a lot cheaper. (The result was the Private Express Statutes giving the government a mail monopoly that still haunts us.)

There were no federal taxes. None. In fact, the income tax was a lifetime into the future. Federal spending was about $3 million per year. That is not a typo. It may seem so now that we are trying to "get used" to federal budgets in the trillions (a million millions), but it is correct: $3,000,000. About fifteen cents per person per year. Needless to say, there was no bureaucracy worth mention, nor any welfarism, nor the ceaseless clamor by interest groups for handouts or privileges. The government had neither the power nor the money to buy votes.

Today the government spends more than a thousand times as much *every day,* and annually charges us something like $5,000 per person—man, woman and child—to do so. If there is any limit whatever on its power and grasp, I do not know it. The only constitutional rule I can think of that is still fully observed is electing two senators from each state. Since 1844, the smallest government in the world has become the largest. Does anybody in his right mind think we are better off because of this? And if not, where did we go astray, and what can we now do about it?

* * *

Never have we so needed to recall our roots.

I do, of course, have a special reason for turning to the perspectives of 1844. In June of that year, a group of Free Will Baptists met in Michigan, newest of the twenty-six states. On the agenda was a resolution for the establishment of a denominational college. The motion was defeated. But a rump session refused to surrender the dream. They had "no endowment, no charter, no legal organization, no buildings, no library, no apparatus, no students."

So, in good American style, Michigan Central College was born within a few months. The new college began life on December 4, 1844, in Spring Arbor, Michigan. Its president and sole faculty member was Daniel McBride Graham, a June graduate of Oberlin College. School convened in a two-room deserted store so decrepit that snow came in through the chinks in the walls. In a few years, the school moved to the little town of Hillsdale and became Hillsdale College, of which I am privileged to be president.

The first class had five students. I feel as if I know them all. Let me tell you about two of them.

One was Clinton Bowen Fisk, a "particularly lively pupil." These were abolitionist times, and Fisk meant to have a full say in ending slavery. He was an early Civil War volunteer, rose quickly in rank, and was a brevetted major general by the war's end. A year later, in 1866, he founded a school for Negroes in an army barracks in Nashville. Whether this was the first such school for freed slaves is unclear, but it was certainly among the first. A year later it was chartered as Fisk University. Before many years, freshmen at Fisk received a classical education, including readings in original Latin and Greek, and Bible studies in Hebrew. Harvard, today, does not even come close. Anyone who now sees limited educability among minorities or among any group is going to hear from me and from Clinton Bowen Fisk.

The other in that first class of five I'd like to mention was Livonia Benedict. She was the first woman in the state to be admitted to a degree program by a Michigan college on a par with men, and went on to be the first woman in Michigan and the second in the nation to earn the coveted Bachelor of Arts degree, in 1852, and the second to earn a degree of any kind. (Her classmate, Elizabeth D. Camp of Palmyra, New York, was the first in the state to win a Bachelor of Science, the year before.) Miss Benedict married the Reverend William Perrine, another Hillsdale graduate. She was a founder of the first auxiliary of the Women's Foreign Missionary Society of Michigan and a leader of the Women's Christian Temperance Union. After her husband died, she endowed a scholarship in the Bareilly Theological Seminary in North India in his name.

Nondiscrimination and true academic freedom were principles carved in stone at Hillsdale, from its inception so long ago. We were graduating women and blacks more than a century before the federal government decided to get into the "equal opportunity" business. In the period 1868 to 1907, we also graduated foreign students (including women) from India, Prussia, England, Persia and Japan, and a full-blooded Cherokee Indian from the Oklahoma Territory (he played guard on the 1893 championship football team). Women have been serving on the Hillsdale Board of Trustees continuously since 1893. Hillsdale was the first college in Michigan, and one of the first in the nation, to elect a female trustee and to employ women as faculty members.

The College had a showdown with federal officiousness as early as World War I. An army lieutenant (a Southerner) ruled that a black student, though otherwise qualified, could not serve in the regular Hillsdale R.O.T.C., but would have to be inducted into a Negro unit. This "touched off a flurry of telegrams between [Hillsdale] President Mauck and a war department committee, resulting in final instructions to [the lieutenant] to follow the age-old Hillsdale practice of treating individuals without regard to color or creed."

But the real crunch came almost sixty years later, in 1975. Sticking to our first principles, we had a ferocious encounter with a federal bureaucratic machine that, in effect, ordered us to practice discrimination by admitting students and hiring faculty on the basis of race and gender. Little Hillsdale said no. We stood alone. We fought. We gave it everything we had. And, after many years of litigation, we lost to sheer federal power. That story follows. It is an eye-opener, especially as to the real purposes of some so-called "civil rights" laws.

Today, legislation to "correct" Hillsdale's insistence on its freedom has become law. What the legislation really attacks is *your* freedom, and in an unprecedented way. It will put you under the

federal bureaucrat's thumb in your farm or factory, your school
board or your city council, your corner store or your church. Its
reach is without limit.

Hillsdale will fight again. But this time, if we must fight alone,
you and all America will lose.

Hillsdale, Michigan   George Roche
September 1990

Chapter I

STANDING FIRM
A True Story—With a Warning for Us All

The letter came as a shock.

I remember well that summer day in 1975 when it arrived. After fifteen years of litigation, legal fees and public discussion, I can say with feeling that nothing has been quite the same since at Hillsdale College. But I am proud of our stand, and can also say that Hillsdale has emerged the stronger for it, and more determined than ever to maintain its independence.

This is the story of what happened when a small private liberal arts college, standing alone, resisted regulation by the vast federal bureaucracy: regulation that would have compromised its academic integrity and freedom. It is a story that ought to alert every American that we each and all must be ready to fight again for our independence. The reach of overweening government power has been extended into every store, office and farm, every school and church, in every corner of America. This is a new, meddlesome, officious use of force, far beyond any governmental powers that our Founding Fathers contemplated. The Founders, indeed, fought and died to free us from just such arbitrary power, and tried to prevent it from ever occurring again, in Jefferson's words, with "the chains of the Constitution." Now our fundamental liberty is, again, very much at stake. The battle Hillsdale has been fighting for fifteen years is a battle which should concern all Americans.

Our story. The letter was from the federal government. To be specific, it was from the Office of Civil Rights of the then Department of Health, Education and Welfare (HEW).

It said: Hillsdale College, as a "recipient institution," must sign a compliance form agreeing to submit information to HEW listing the sexual and ethnic makeup of our school.

This is obnoxious. The student's race and gender are of no concern to the educator. To the contrary, one function of a liberal arts education is to overcome such invidious distinctions and to promote a civilized, color-blind, harmonious order. This ideal was very widely shared until recent times and has always been the rule at Hillsdale.

At its founding in 1844, Hillsdale threw open its doors to anyone of any race, creed or nationality. It was established by men and women "grateful to God for the inestimable blessings" of religious and civil liberty and "believing that the diffusion of learning is essential to the perpetuity of these blessings." It was their goal "to furnish all persons who wish, irrespective of nation, color, or sex a literary and scientific education," and to combine with this such moral "and social instruction as will best develop the mind and improve the hearts of its pupils." Hillsdale was educating women and free slaves on an equal basis before the Civil War—more than a century before there were any federal bureaucrats to tell us what the "right" ethnic or gender composition of a school should be. In those days this was quite a radical stance. But we meant it then and we mean it just as much today when the civilized ideal is again under attack from bureaucracy. Genuine education focuses on the individual and does not admit of any such quotas. It is open to all—and it always has been at Hillsdale.

And Hillsdale a *"recipient institution"*? Absurd. Since its founding, Hillsdale has *never* accepted a penny of federal funding—which makes it all but unique among colleges these days. (Don't even ask about the big universities.) From the beginning our Trustees have always been aware that nothing comes dearer than "free" money. The school has felt all along that we would surrender our academic freedom by taking any such funding, and we have always refused even to consider it.

Whatever did these bureaucrats mean, we were a "recipient" of federal funds? Naturally, I thought at first it must be a mistake. Bureaucracies, especially very big ones, *have* been known to make mistakes. (HEW at the time "ranked" as the third largest government in the world, behind only the Soviet state and the U.S. government as a whole.)

It was not a mistake. The bureaucratic reasoning was that, although Hillsdale did not take any federal funds, some of its students had government loans or grants. The students spent some of this money paying for their education. That made Hillsdale a "recipient" too.

If you think this reasoning is cockeyed, that makes two of us. By the same logic, every fast food franchise, laundry and bookstore in Hillsdale, Michigan, would be equally a "recipient institution," and thus be put under the bureaucratic thumb. It goes a lot further than this. Think of the countless millions who receive Social Security checks, food stamps, Medicare, grants and other federal benefits. Every place they spend anything becomes, equally, a "recipient institution." In effect, every place of business in America, down to the last lemonade stand, would be subject to bureaucratic control.

So ran my thoughts and fears. A dozen years later it is all the law of the land. How we came to this appalling situation is part of our story.

The form, said HEW, was required under Title IX of the Education Act Amendments of 1972, which barred discrimination based on sex. HEW would then determine in bureaucratic fashion if we were meeting the gender requirements for this particular act.

I remind you, it was never shown or even alleged that we were discriminating against anyone or violating any laws. We were not defendants. The only point of this maneuver was to put us under federal regulation.

The same form, or something of the sort, went out to every institution of higher education in the country. Almost all of them dutifully complied: because almost all of them are avid diners at the federal trough, or, more politely, "recipient institutions." Does anyone remember that, when federal aid to education was being debated in the 1960s, its opponents were jeered out of the arena for arguing that federal aid meant federal control? That academic freedom was at stake? The loudest jeering was precisely from those institutions most eager for the money: the ones now snarled in government red tape.

There were at least a few schools left, however, that cared more about education than about federal slops. A bare handful of these, we learned later, did not fill out the HEW compliance form. But neither did they announce their noncompliance to HEW. They hoped matters would fall through a crack in our Byzantine bureaucracy and never be noticed. (And for a time they were right about that.)

So it was that Hillsdale was the only college in America to notify the government in the fall of 1975 that it would not sign the compliance form. Hillsdale alone took a stand, stood up to HEW, and said *"No.* And we are prepared to make a legal issue of it."

* * *

We stood alone for several years. Ours was the lone voice raised to insist that the government's definition of a recipient institution was wrong. It had changed the definition to one that defied all sense. The old definition was simply an institution that received federal funds. The new one was radically different: any institution having on its campus any *individual* who received a federal grant or loan. This would extend bureaucratic power into countless areas it had no business. It was wrong.

Our position was clear: We had never accepted funds from the government, so we were under no obligation to divulge proprietary information. In this we were by no means objecting to government civil rights policy per se. For us, the issue had nothing to do with civil rights or affirmative action. Nor was our record in civil rights ever in question. Rather, we were convinced that if we complied with the HEW order we would be unjustly liable to future regulation. This would mean abandoning Hillsdale's long-standing and cherished independence from government support and interference.

The agency countered that because some Hillsdale students

received student loans and scholarships, the college was an "indirect" recipient of federal funds, and, therefore, obligated to comply. This was exactly why we were objecting. There was no point in discussing it any further.

We took it to court.

Several years later Grove City College, which is affiliated with the Presbyterian Church, came under similar bureaucratic pressure. It was enjoined by the government to submit the compliance form. Grove City, like Hillsdale, had never taken any federal funds. They approached us for information and help in their defense and we were able to provide substantial documentation to aid them in preparing their case.

From that point the two cases wound through different paths in the federal appeals court circuits. Hillsdale eventually won a partial victory in the Sixth Circuit. The appeals court ruled that, while federal loans and grants did make Hillsdale an indirect recipient of federal funds, the federal regulation was too broad and could not cover the whole institution.

Meanwhile, Grove City suffered defeat in the Second Circuit. In a way this set the stage for the resolution of both cases. The government chose not to appeal the Hillsdale decision. Instead, it concentrated on Grove City. The path was thus cleared for Grove City's case to be heard by the Supreme Court. Ironically, the legal battle Hillsdale had undertaken almost a decade earlier finally came to national attention as the case of *Grove City* v *Bell* (named for then-Secretary of Education Terrel H. Bell).

In February 1984, the Supreme Court ruled that any American college or university was the recipient of federal funds if loans and grants were received by a *single* student on its campus. The government, however, could withhold funds only from specific departments or programs which were not in compliance with federal regulations. In other words, the statutory powers were again found to be too broad. This was essentially the same decision Hillsdale had received earlier in the Sixth Circuit Court of Appeals.

* * *

The Supreme Court ruling was a blow to academic freedom. It gave the government an enormous amount of economic leverage with

Hillsdale College
Hillsdale, Michigan

Resolution

WHEREAS the Board of Trustees of Hillsdale College has been made aware of new restrictive regulations imposed by the Department of Health, Education and Welfare promulgated under the guise of implementing Title IX of the Education Amendments of 1972; and

WHEREAS Hillsdale College has maintained its freedom and independence of federal control by consistent refusal of federal aid to education, federal grants and any and all forms of subsidy by the Federal government; and

WHEREAS, by the regulations aforementioned, the Federal government now seeks to impose its control over such freedom and independence through the subterfuge that a few of the students of Hillsdale College receive federal aid through the medium of such programs as Veterans Benefits and the National Direct Student Loan Fund; and

WHEREAS it is the conviction of the Board of Trustees of Hillsdale College that such regulations are excessive of the authority granted by Congress and violative of the inalienable rights of freedom and choice of this institution and are therefore immoral and illegal; and

WHEREAS Hillsdale College has traditionally far exceeded the social benefit purported to be achieved in such regulations by natural and voluntary non-discrimination: Now therefore be it

RESOLVED, That Hillsdale College will hold to its traditional philosophy of equal opportunity without discrimination by reason of race, religion or sex, but such non-discrimination will be voluntary, thus preserving equality with dignity and encouraging friendship based on recognition of equal worth and mutual respect; and be it

RESOLVED further, That Hillsdale College will, to the extent of its meager resources and with the help of God, resist by all legal means this and all other encroachments on its freedom and independence.

THE BOARD OF TRUSTEES OF
HILLSDALE COLLEGE

Donald R. Mossey
Chairman

George Charles Roche III
President

Adopted October 10, 1975

which to control the internal affairs of educational institutions—even those not receiving funds directly.

This was intolerable to a school that had fiercely guarded its independence for 140 years. The decision had a profound effect on Hillsdale. We met and discussed and agonized. There was only one way out left to us. We seized it, grateful that we still had the freedom to do so, however painful the price. The trustees resoundingly reaffirmed our private status and our stand against government intervention. They vowed to resist any such intrusions to the full extent of Hillsdale's resources. Their resolution is reproduced on the opposite page.

In June 1985, Hillsdale announced that it would no longer accept students who intended to pay for any part of their college education with federal grants and loans.

We informed the government that no student listing Hillsdale as the school of matriculation should be given a federal grant or loan, because we could not accept that student. We then notified our parents and students that if they needed financial assistance for education, we would do what we could to find private dollars to make it possible for them to attend Hillsdale.

Most colleges at the time were relying more and more on government aid to their students, for tuition and other expenses. And as federal grants and loans to students were rising sharply, tuitions were also rising sharply. Supply and demand works in the groves of academe as well as it works everywhere else. We were painfully aware of these trends and what they would cost us, but that only made us the more resolved to resist. When we said no, we meant it for once and for all. Hillsdale's stand did not go unnoticed.

The *Wall Street Journal* commended us, noting that "President Roche has in effect replied to HEW's quota overtures the same as General McAuliffe replied to German demands that he surrender at Bastogne ('Nuts!')."

Economist Milton Friedman commented in *Newsweek*, " . . . they have with clear conscience regarded themselves as not subject to HEW control."

Writing in *Fortune*, Irving Kristol observed, "Hillsdale, a small, traditional and generally excellent liberal arts college, refuses on principle to accept any government funds. Roche is therefore free to speak up, as most other college presidents are not—and he does." (I'm afraid Irving has my number.)

The *Indianapolis Star* concluded: "So hurrah for Hillsdale! If the ever-expanding grasp of federal intervention in the lives of private citizens and institutions is to be turned back, it will be by just such determination to stand and fight."

Needless to say, we were much cheered by this enthusiastic response. It was welcome proof that Hillsdale would no longer stand alone; that many share our concern about the lengthening reach of bureaucratic coercion in the field of education and in our private lives. But of course Hillsdale's immediate problem required more than moral support. Now we had to find the funds to back up our pledge to aid our students.

To this vital need the response was all the more gratifying, and translated into tangible support for our Freedom Fund. Over $30 million in contributions came from individuals and organizations who endorsed and aided Hillsdale's determination to remain private. That support proved all the more that a national leadership community is committed, as we are, to the traditional, private ways to get things done.

Despite this impressive outpouring of public generosity, the problems we face have only been blunted, not solved. The reason is easy to find. In providing financial aid for our students, we are forced to compete with the biggest money machine in all human history: the U.S. government. This is like David versus one hundred Goliaths. Federal aid to students is skyrocketing. You have been hearing otherwise from the media since 1980 and the story you have heard is simply not true. If you have heard college and university presidents whining about how the administration has gutted higher education, you heard no more than the usual pleadings of panhandlers. All this is nonsense. The federal government is pouring money—your money, I might add—into student aid. Today, three out of every four dollars of need-based student aid come from federal programs. Tuitions soar to soak up all this nice "free" money, creating new pressures to raise student aid to even higher levels. But the level of education does not rise at all. Somehow, all those billions drift away into urgent "administrative" budgets and are lost to education. Bureaucracy breeds bureaucracy.

What this means for us is trying to match that torrent of tax monies, dollar for dollar, for the students who need financial aid to attend Hillsdale. In the first three years of our program, our outlays nearly *tripled*. Does that tell you something about federal spending? And the burden is growing almost daily.

If this seems too abstract, let me give you a down-to-earth human example of what it means. Not long ago I had to report to the trustees about 27 students whom we had accepted and who were committed to come to Hillsdale. The gist of my report was that these were all quality students, the very sort we like to see. They all had good academic credentials. They wanted to attend Hillsdale. We offered them the best aid package we could afford—and lost them. Other schools, with the help of tax dollars, could offer far more aid than we could. It isn't that other schools could offer more of their own resources. They couldn't. The fact is, they are committing a very small amount of their own resources, compared to our commitment. The other schools, however, had the advantage of being able to pick the pockets of taxpayers for their package. That we *will not* do. It does put us at a disadvantage, and we did lose some promising students. But we sleep nights.

The problem is only going to get worse—for everyone, not just for Hillsdale—until we all say "no." As things stand, enormous amounts of money flow to the "higher education" factories that are losing all sense of what an education is. In this, the students are the first and hardest-hit victims. Not only can they be cheated out of a real education, they will be stuck with an ever-increasing bill for all that nice, easy grant and loan money they were given in order to attend. For the last few private schools that struggle to survive and preserve the liberal arts tradition, the invasion of federal funds is nothing but trouble. How are we to compete with the power of taxation? We try, but with increasingly demanding measures. Yet we few who fight the battle alone keep alive and uphold the proud tradition of private education.

Think about this. *All* higher education in America was once private. All of it was established by groups with religious affiliations who freely gave their energies and resources so that education might be open to anyone. The trend has long been in the other direction, of course: toward huge, secular, tax-supported, bureaucratically approved universities. Think about this, too, as you contemplate what everybody knows to be true: Bureaucratic ("public") management of education goes up and up; the quality of education goes down and down. Surprise again! But did anyone ever really expect bureaucrats to be educators, or even to know why such a thing as a liberal arts education should exist? Would you buy your bread from a bakery that had never handled flour? That is precisely the kind of thinking that turns education over to bureaucrats.

There are more than a thousand birds, beasts and bugs on the endangered species list. None is remotely as close to extinction as traditional private education. If and when the last vestiges of private purpose and charity and skills in education are shot down, education itself must fall. For education is a continuing process, a transmission of knowledge and values from generation to generation. When the last real schools are gone, who will educate the next generation of educators? The U.S. Department of Education? Forget it.

In a word, Hillsdale is fighting for its life. Don't take me amiss; we are not going to fold up the day after tomorrow for lack of funds. Money, as I have said, is an increasing problem in competition with tax funding, but it will be a good while before we have to move to the intensive care unit. No, the real question is whether this country is going to offer educational opportunity to all. To do this, we have to go on providing the real item in the only setting that still can sustain it: the private college.

What I, and the trustees, and all of us at Hillsdale fear is the next invasion of bureaucratic power. The one that will say in effect: "Never mind that you are a private institution, we are taking over now." There is no legal way for this to happen yet. But what new legislation will be written? Thanks to its stand, Hillsdale is a prime target. Already discussed in bureaucratic memoranda is the idea that tax exemption is really a loss of government revenue: as if the government already *owned* all of our earnings, and merely lets us keep some at its own pleasure. This is a complete inversion of property rights and due process. It may also be argued that deductions for religion, charity, education or other high-minded activities are no longer valid, because the government itself provides all such services. (Insane, but power-wielders and their friends are not very fussy about how they reduce private life to subjection.) Finally, I suspect the argument will be raised that private education has religious overtones and is therefore in violation of the famous "wall of separation" between church and state that doesn't happen to exist in the Constitution. When arguments sink this low, there will be no further point in referring to the Constitution or to the law at all. We will be ruled by naked power.

It is foolish to shelve these concerns, thinking "we'll cross that bridge when we come to it." I believe it is only a matter of time until another assault is mounted against Hillsdale and private education in general. We must be ready for it. At Hillsdale, we are already building our defenses. It is grating to have to do so. What harm has one small college done to the Republic that it should be subject to such attack? We have done no wrong except in the eyes of those who demand that government control every detail of life. To them, Hillsdale's independence is insolent defiance of their power and designs. And they have a point. We will remain defiant.

If you think my concerns are exaggerated or overblown, read on. The story isn't over.

* * *

The Supreme Court's decision in *Grove City* v. *Bell* did not, as one might expect, please liberal legislators. In truth, they were furious that they had not quite reduced private colleges to unconditional surrender. There was that one last small loophole, that an entire institution could not be brought to account for some violation in one of its departments or programs. Bullying one department would not do; the point is to bully the whole school.

They promptly whipped up the Civil Rights Restoration Act, a bill to "correct the defects" in the enforcement of Title IX of the Education Amendments of 1972. The principal sponsor was Senator Ted Kennedy. What the bill provides is that the government may cut all funds to any institution that fails to fully comply with a regulation—in even one department. It applies to any direct or *indirect* recipient of federal funds.

This certainly "corrects" the loophole. It is also, in my opinion, one of the most sweeping impositions of federal power over free Americans that has ever been seriously proposed. Note well its means of enforcement: "Toe our line or we'll take away your funds." It is scarcely possible to pose a more naked threat. They might as well announce, "You take our money, we *own* you." With this, America's great experiment in self-government has lost its last battle. This kind of absolutism is cut from the cloth of the tyrannies of the Old World, whose peoples were not citizens but subjects with no basic rights. What is especially galling about this is that "federal" money was forcibly extracted from us in the first place. When they "give" some of it back, it comes not with strings attached but with chains.

Things get very much worse. The law targets all *indirect* recipients of federal funds. That means corner stores that take food stamps. That means churches that feed the poor in programs with even minimal federal connection. That means every American in any economic activity whatever. There is no way to prevent "federal" dollars from entering the operation somehow. It was argued: "Oh, no, the law wasn't meant to go *this* far; we will always use a 'narrow' interpretation." But the law *does* go this far. And the power will be used. I don't think there is a case in history when government, given such power, has not ultimately used it.

The false definition of "recipient institution" that we at Hillsdale tried so hard to fight in 1975 now comes back to haunt all of America.

Even in a "narrow" application, the law is an affront to even-handed justice. Where the blind goddess of justice was once supposed to view all who appeared before her with impartiality, now she peeks. "Tell me your race, your creed and your sex," she says, "and I will tell you how I will treat you." This is not justice. It *is* racism, it *is* sexism.

The Civil Rights Restoration Act floated around Congress for four years. I wrote a number of articles warning about it, from

Hillsdale's firsthand experience in the case. These were heard in some circles, but rejected with scorn in Congress. The magic words, "Civil Rights," have a dazzling effect. Legislators hardly dare vote against anything labeled "Civil Rights." But the label was utterly false. The bill had nothing to do with restoring civil rights. Remember that the two schools involved, Hillsdale and Grove City College, had never been accused of any civil rights violations in the first place. The issue was the reach of federal power. The bill "corrected" our minor victory with an extension of federal power, plain and simple—and on an unprecedented scale.

The Act was passed in 1988. President Reagan vetoed it, infuriating its liberal sponsors even more. Both houses of Congress provided the large majorities necessary to override the veto. The Civil Rights Restoration Act is now law.

How bad is this law? Let me give you the barest taste of its potential. Due to a recent court ruling, alcoholics, drug addicts and transvestites are categorized as "handicapped" and are thus protected under the Civil Rights Act. Ponder this all-too-possible scenario: A drug addict applies for a job at a pharmacy. The pharmacy, which accepts Medicare and Medicaid payments via its clientele, cannot turn down this "handicapped" applicant. It is required to comply with the federal regulations, even if it is aghast at turning a junkie loose in its supplies of drugs. Moreover, every other pharmacy in the same "geographic area" (also defined by government) is then obliged to submit to regulations also. There is quite literally no limit to the number or scope of similar cases that may affect us (and probably will). The law is wide open. About anything you can imagine may be a future civil rights case.

One hardly knows whether to laugh or scream. There is an impish libertarian streak in me that longs to say: "Do it! Make good your threat. Withhold your funds from all the colleges and great universities. Pull the plug on teachers' unions. Bankrupt all the busybodies and do-gooders. Do it!" Can you imagine the likes of Dartmouth or Berkeley getting kicked off the trough? The prospect is so delicious that taxpayers might form posses to track down civil rights violations in every recipient institution in the land.

The civil rights restorers didn't really mean they would disinherit *Harvard*—did they? The point is, no matter what they "meant," the power and *responsibility* to enforce civil rights regulations by withholding funds from violators is now the law. By all the canons of justice, the law must be equitably and fully enforced. Moreover, the status of civil rights enforcement is so loose and capricious that almost any slight (whether real or unintended) to a member of a legally protected group can be construed a violation of federal law. Woe to the institution in which some unwary freshman gapes at the transvestite sociology professor snorting cocaine. His (or is it "her"?) civil rights have been violated, and the institution is held responsible. Off with its funds! Yes, Harvard too.

What began (let us allow) with the best of intentions, the decent impulse to protect the weak, the needy, the handicapped, has evolved into a federal bulldozer to flatten the rights of all Americans. No business or organization, profit-making or not-for profit; no school or church; no local government is safe from vague federal fishing expeditions—or outright threats—to "enforce civil rights." Where it will all end, no one knows. I do know this is the price we invariably pay when we allow government coercion to replace all the bonds of reason and sympathy that join us together in civilized society. Will we ever learn, with Lord Acton, that power corrupts, and absolute power corrupts absolutely?

Hillsdale has taken its stand. If need be, we will fight again. We will defend ourselves, as best we can, by distancing ourselves from governmental reach, whether that is intended to harm or (God forbid) help us. As best we can, we will build our resources in hopes of surviving the next assault and carrying on our work: liberal arts education. It may be that we will be swept away in the flood; but we do not, as Canon Bell reminded us, have to sing Hosannahs to the river gods.

What will you do? I said earlier that if little Hillsdale has to go it alone this time, all America will lose. Perhaps at first reading that claim sounded a bit self-inflated. Do you see now what I mean?

Chapter II

WHO CAN DO THE JOB?

This book reasserts, as strongly as I am able, the role, power and leadership of the individual person and the private, voluntary institutions through which he chooses to function. It is about reclaiming our lives and hopes from the never-never land of power and politics. It is about the failure of leadership in our time, why it has failed, and how to put things right. Mostly it is about us; for only you and I can overcome the obstacles that have been put before us: and restore life on a human scale. Nobody can do it for us. Certainly politicians can't do it for us. Politics is most of the problem.

We have long been told that the affairs of mankind are too vast and too complicated for you and me to understand. In a dozen ways, we are led to believe that the individual is nothing and the group is everything. We are likened to identical bees in a hive, or interchangeable cogs in a machine, or statistical units in a system, or corks in the sea, tossed about by vast forces we cannot control. The message is always the same: the individual is powerless, the system or society or state is all-powerful. When things go wrong, "society" or "the system" is to blame. The individual has no responsibility.

I am here to tell you that the individual is the primary human reality. Everything that is conceived and accomplished is done by individuals. All human power resides in the individual. Insofar as we have been led to think anything else, we have been sold a bill of goods by ideologues and social engineers.

We are bombarded by such notions as society, race, class, gender, public and countless other groupings like them. To one school of thought, these aggregates are as real as the gods were to the Greeks, and they even get a definite article: *the* working class, *the* people. However, the concepts are all fictions. They are abstract ideas; sometimes convenient ideas, perhaps, but they have no real existence. They cannot be defined, except in the vaguest, most arbitrary generalities. There is virtually nothing one can say about any of them that is true. Try it. Any statement you can make about a large aggregate of human beings will be either so sweeping as to be meaningless or so full of exceptions that it is not true. Are all Caucasians white? Of course not. Can we even distinguish between a working class and an ownership class, as Karl Marx tried to? Not in this country, where millions of "workers" own stock, often in the company they work for. Can you complete the following to make true statements that add to knowledge? "All Americans are . . . "; "Society is . . . ." Please do not send me your answers. One cannot possibly know, or say much of anything useful about, such large internally diverse groupings.

Nor do we spend much time thinking of ourselves as certified members of this or that aggregation. Even less do we try to act as if we were members. Does anyone get up in the morning and ask himself, "How am I going to schedule my day so as to be a member of the upper-middle class?" He couldn't do it if he tried: there are no exclusively upper-middle class characteristics upon which to model behavior.

Nor yet does our alleged membership in any supposed group matter very much to us compared to the overall concerns of life. When you think about it, we spend relatively little time fussing about whether we are black/white, male/female, American/French, or any other group-think category. Such things are just little bits of our life, and if we made more of them we would be called obsessed. You and I, for instance, love America, but we could hardly spend 365 days a year being "patriotic." Being "religious" does not mean spending all our hours in church, and concern about our children's education does not take us to a PTA meeting every day. We are but part-time "members" of any grouping, and the larger the group, the smaller its claim on our attention. Our true concerns lie much closer: in our home and family and work and friends and community life. Even our abiding patriotism is a reflection of the fact that in America, we remain free to do the homey things that really matter to us.

For these reasons, *it is impossible to infer any knowledge of the individual from the characteristics of the group.* I put that in italics because it is essential that we understand it. Ignoring or denying this truth has contributed heavily to most of our problems in America today. Understanding it is a key to finding the way home. Surely it is the beginning of wisdom to know what is and what is not possible for us to know. Otherwise we will build our house on sand. Frank Chodorov used to growl, "Society *are* people." Sane public policy must begin with the understanding that the public *are* diverse, self-responsible individuals.

This truth is forgotten in all the studies and polls and statistics we see in such abundance. We may learn something from polls and statistics, but only about arbitrary groupings, not about a given individual in the group. We won't even learn much about the group: human beings cannot be reduced to numbers. You and I, as individuals, are immune to being put under microscopes. Science can study only things that can be repeated; it cannot study a one-time thing, a human life.

This truth is not so much forgotten as trampled by all the collectivist schemes that have bedeviled our times. The perpetrators of these schemes, to a man, believe that they can say what any person is, because he is (and they invent the terms that will follow) a proletarian, a capitalist, a Jew, a Nazi, a member of society, a white Anglo-Saxon Protestant upper-upper-middle-class liberal Democrat male from Westchester County, New York. You can invent categories all day long, but they never tell you what a person really is. They say nothing about our inner feelings and hopes, our moral fortitude or character, our sacrifices and devotion and love. They say nothing about anything that matters.

We are, God bless us, individuals all: each of us unique in mind and body, the only one of us there will ever be. It is a scientific certainty that no two of us are quite alike. To lump us together is adding apples and oranges—and kumquats. This is not possible in mathematics. Calling any sum of us a class or race or giant fruit salad is no more helpful in human affairs. We are not races and classes and genders; we are persons who come into this world and who leave it one at a time. That is the reality. That is what we are, how we act.

* * *

What harm is there, it will be objected, to seeing, indeed seeking, the connections that link us to political, social, racial or economic groups? My answer is that there should be no harm, and will be none, so long as we distinguish carefully between the reality and the illusion. We humans, going back to Genesis, are born namers and classifiers: this is how we build our science. Obviously our efforts to classify this group or that and to learn something of its tendencies is on solid academic and moral ground. There are plenty of commercial uses for this sort of study as well.

But there are many thinkers who do not make that critical distinction between the concrete reality of the individual and the squishy generalities of the group. On the contrary, the whole trend of modern thought—not least in many an American university—is to put things exactly backward: the group is held to be the primary entity, the person is at best a statistical unit or cell in some larger body, or worse, a beast to be used or destroyed as rulers see fit. As the joke has it, "I love humanity. It's people I can't stand." It's a good joke, but if the idea is taken seriously and given political power, it is a recipe for totalitarianism. Ideas, as I never tire of saying, have consequences, and that goes for bad ones as well as good ones. This one, turning the natural order of things upside-down, has devastated much of the world for much of this century.

This type of thinking readily turns into a quasi-religion. It attracts dreamers who dream about these fictitious groups and say to themselves, "I see how everybody behaves *because* they are members of these groups that I have conceived. But I could run things better. There would be peace and harmony and justice in this world if they would just do what J tell them to. I would create a New Man and make the world clean." Right. And they probably glow in the dark hearing that old tune, "To Dream the Impossible Dream."

At this point we pass from an intellectual mistake to what was known a few centuries ago—that I have to dust off the word is a measure of their success—as heresy. They say God was wrong and they can do better. The dreamers have lost not only all sense of reality, but their conscience. They think they know something about group members, but they do not. That is the intellectual mistake. But they also think they know better than God, or you, or me, or anyone else, what is right and just for each of our lives. That is a moral outrage and a threat to all.

Think about it. You arrange your life to make the best you can of your circumstances. Chances are you are reasonably content with your lot, and you have worked hard to get where you are. What are you going to do when some radical academic says that your whole life—your aspirations, your family life, your work, your hopes—is a bad thing and that you are a nothing who is getting in the way of his utopia? Are you going to cave in and become his slavering servant?

Few ever do. We are born free, and know we are free. All collectivist schemes founder on the same reef. They cannot make us be what we are not; and we are not slaves. It is in their confrontation with the human reality that the dreamers without conscience turn vicious. If we do not choose to be what they want us to be, they will compel us. If they cannot compel us, even at gunpoint, they will "eliminate" for the "good of the people." They will call us false names—reactionaries, capitalists, imperialists, bourgeois, Jews, or anything "evil-sounding" that serves their purposes. Next come concentration camps, or machine guns chattering before a mass grave, or a canister of Zyklon-B in the gas chamber. I know, nothing like this has happened to us in America, and I don't think it will. But the profound evil of those ideas and their tragic results are recent history. Genocidal war against civilization is the logical consequence of both the modernist philosophies and collectivist politics, as I have written elsewhere.* False ideas are to blame for this history, and our only defense against them here is knowing the

---

*A World Without Heroes, Hillsdale College Press, 1987

right ideas. We are not immune. We have ourselves been placed on the path to disaster by do-everything government, the politicization of our lives and an obscene tax burden to pay for it all.

Should we go on dreaming, I propose a modest experiment. Try to change your spouse into someone new and better, and let me know how you succeed. If you can manage that, *and* bring up a perfect family, you *may* be ready to reform your brother-in-law too. After that we can talk about changing the whole world. But by then we will have learned that we are not called on to change the world. Our only task, as Albert Jay Nock put it, is to "present society with one improved unit"—ourselves.

Reality, I say again, is the person. Categories of people are fictitious and trivial. What we can really know is what is ourselves and what is close to us. Nobody knows who we are or what we want out of life better than you and I do. Nobody else can run our life for us. And nobody, as economist Milton Friedman likes to note, can spend your money better or more carefully than you. We may be, will be, thwarted in our tasks time and again by those who would compel us to fit their fantasies and be what we are not. But we will not be denied. Our lives are our own. Uncle Sugar and Big Brother cannot do for us what we must do ourselves.

But we needn't dwell on the obstacles before us. There is lots of good news to report on what individuals like us have done in the face of adversity, by means you and I can use as well.

My special concern as president of a small private college is, needless to say, better education. Education is, at the last, transmitting the moral and religious values from one generation to the next. In case you haven't been paying attention, this is illegal in public schools, and the laws are vigorously enforced. You were wondering what is wrong with the schools? Why your children and mine don't emerge triumphant from twelve years of mandatory state schooling? What they usually get is twelve years of indoctrination into collectivist fantasies. It gets worse in higher education.

Little Hillsdale is not like that at all. In our school, we try to our utmost to teach the students who come to us, one at a time. We recognize and applaud their individuality, and do all that we can to bring out what they, each on his own merits, can be. This, I firmly believe, is what education should be. We are not in business to teach members of alleged groups—nor was any real educational institution, ever. Education is nothing if not the teaching of one person at a time.

Hillsdale may be a homely example, but it is one near and dear to me, and one I *know* is done right. Hillsdale attracts wonderful young people. It gives them the full value of education. I do not say so as salemanship (although you or your children, if qualified, are most welcome), but to remind you that this task can be done well. As you will learn in more detail, Hillsdale has paid dearly to maintain its rights to do things well. But we still get things done, and there are avenues open to you, too, to get things done. It is all a matter of insisting on our liberty, accepting our responsibility, and showing our leadership. You and I have to take charge. We are, one by one, everything that matters, and we are, one by one, responsible for tomorrow.

Chapter III
THE IDEAS OF TOMORROW
Reflections on the Reagan Era

It is good to turn back to our roots at times, especially when we are confused about current matters or at some turning point in our lives. This is as true for a nation as it is for a person. Let me say a very few words about my own background to introduce a subject of common interest.

I grew up in the mountains of Colorado. My home was in a little valley called Chalk Creek Gulch, all but lost between two of the great peaks forming a part of the Continental Divide. Elementary education for me was in an eight-grade, one-room schoolhouse five miles away at Gas Creek. Most of the pupils who attended Gas Creek School were from ranching families in the area. One of those families, the Clines, had nine children. By the time I was in the eighth grade with the eldest of the Cline children, Darryl and Virgelene, the youngest of the Clines, the twins, Leonard and Lionel, had entered first grade—of course, putting all of us together in the same classroom. In that year there were sixteen children in Gas Creek School, and nine of them were Clines. I don't know what you know about country schools, but I assure you this situation had a profound effect on playground dynamics.

I mention my rustic upbringing to suggest something about growing up in a simpler, surer America that now seems lost and far away—but only seems so. It is not lost. Nor is that time so far behind us that we cannot turn to it for wise counsel.

In the 1940s, when I was growing up there, the valley was a cultural cul-de-sac where things hadn't changed much. People earned their way and spent their lives much as their parents or grandparents had in the 1800s. The automobile, radio, the telephone and such had arrived, of course, but they really hadn't had much of an impact. Why, indeed, should inventions change the things that matter? Folks still raised their children and made their livelihood as they always had. They were churchgoers for the most part, who worshipped unashamed, and honored the Sabbath. They honored their community, their families, their personal obligations and their country as their forefathers had. They knew there was something called Washington, D.C., but it didn't much affect them. They just minded their own business.

In case that sounds hopelessly nostalgic, I am here to tell you it was true. Nor was this way of life, this understanding of life, limited to some little backwater place that time forgot like Chalk Creek Gulch. This was the normal life shared by nearly all Americans. Across the country, in small towns and cities, even in the well-defined neighborhoods of the great metropolises, this was the way things were in the 1940s and into the 1950s. But there was more to it than that. It was in essence the life Americans had shared since the beginnings of the Republic and even before that, in the five generations of colonial life.

What makes all this sound odd—and makes me sound like an old codger ready for a sunny porch and an afghan, I suppose—is the explosion of change in the turbulent 1960s and the troubled 1970s. But you don't have to be old to remember. From the sedate and even prim "bobby sox" era of the forties and fifties, we went to radical student uprisings, race riots, demonstrations in favor of our enemy in Vietnam, the "counterculture," hippies, drugs and the rest of it, in perhaps ten years. Historically, that's a blink of an eye. My point, here, is not to trace the reasons for all this (we will have a clear, hard look later), but to record what dumbfounding changes these were in so short a time. And to make one observation: this set of changes is what is so abnormal and cancerous in America.

It is only with that understanding that we can approach the "Reagan revolution" of the 1980s and what it meant, and means. Whatever else may be said, the Reagan phenomenon was the protest of immemorial America against the immense and often maddening changes of the 1960s and 1970s. It was a protest from our souls: from the time when we all knew who we were and where we were going. Our message was just this: "Enough! We've veered far enough in this crazy direction. It is time to put things right, and make America whole again."

Did the Reagan revolution succeed in this? It had success in important ways. But if you were looking for victory in the same sense as in World War II—unconditional surrender—no, it did not. Nor could it ever have been total victory, for instructive reasons that we must consider.

I am not going to discuss particulars of the Reagan years, for we want to arrive at enduring principles and to answer the key question: Where do we go from here? I think something more important will follow the Reagan revolution. We all have to understand it and play a part in it to determine what we are going to do with our lives and what we can expect from our country.

But it may be said in a general way that the greater Reagan successes came early and followed two avenues. The first avenue involved major restorations of basic rights and freedoms. We had, notably, a sharp reduction in tax rates (that let us keep more of our own money), and deregulation (restoring freedom of trade in at least some businesses that had been pinned under bureaucratic thumbs).

The second avenue was a redefining of government's function back toward normality: that is, with basic emphasis on national defense and justice. The critics' incessant charges that these changes were at the expense of so-called welfare spending were, I am very sorry to say, untrue. Welfare mushroomed at its usual rate, with all the pain that this entails for a growing dependent class with no more hope in life than the next government handout. But at least the perception of what government is supposed to do (and not supposed to do, which is far more important) did change a bit. Not enough, but some. In the original American scheme of things, which survived largely intact into living memory, the government was supposed to mind its own puny and insignificant business and not run everyone else's lives. "That government is best which governs least," said the author of the Declaration of Independence, Thomas Jefferson. Those "do-gooders" who moved us away from that principle—almost to its opposite in recent decades—were wrong. I only wish the Reagan revolution had made more progress in restoring it. But as the bills came due for all the heavy-handed social experiments, and with a different view vigorously expressed by President Reagan, we did begin to see the wisdom of limited, constitutional government again.

Little "revolution" was evident in Mr. Reagan's second term. What more could we really expect? Not only was he a lame duck, but both houses of Congress were in the control of the opposition party. Or more precisely, in the control of a wholly different philosophy of government: the do-everything government America voters tried to stop with their two Reagan landslides. But the damage had been done long since. By usurpation of power over long years, the do-everything view of government entrenched itself to *resist* the wishes of the electorate, and democracy be damned. How else can you describe the gerrymandering and vote-buying that returns *98.4 percent* of incumbent congressmen to Washington? In a fair contest, presumably the split would be nearer 50–50. So, despite a huge Reagan electoral majority, we could not succeed in making our wishes prevail.

I wasn't the least bit surprised. Were you?

I wasn't disappointed, either. I have never expected to achieve anything fundamentally worthwhile through politics. We cannot vote ourselves rich. Politics cannot build or create; it can only rearrange existing wealth (certainly not least into the hands of politicians and their friends). It can't even do that without a more-than-offsetting disincentive to those who *do* produce. Nor can it rob Peter to bribe Paul without a fundamental injustice. Those who work should be able to keep what they earn instead of having it taxed away and given to nonproducers or, worse, to politically favored groups.

In any case, and whatever its specific achievements or failures in policy, the Reagan revolution is effectively over at this writing.

Neither party seems much interested in reviving it, so it seems safe to regard it as history, regardless of the election results to come. All this may sound pessimistic, but it isn't and, as you'll soon see, we have much reason for optimism.

To show you what I mean, let me ask one question. How "revolutionary" was this Reagan revolution, even when it was going full speed? I remind you that there are severely limiting factors on any real changes in Washington or in the country. For example, there's an enormous bureaucracy all but locked in place. It was just as much there and immovable at the end of the Reagan presidency as it was at the beginning. In fact, it continued to grow during the Reagan years. You simply cannot set aside fifty years of big government and expect to get rid of entrenched agencies "just like that." It does not matter which candidate is elected, on what platform. It is a lot harder to dismantle a bureau than to create one in the first place. Every law that gives the government a new power also sets up a new bureau—and my, how they grow! Once a bureau is in place, it has its own interest group clamoring for its continued existence and expansion. Therefore, even in the most promising circumstances, it will take many years and a powerful national consensus to cut the bureaucracy down to size.

Do we have such a consensus? I think we do in the country at large, but Washington, D.C. isn't listening. Did we, at the beginning of the Reagan administration? You and I *knew* it, given the election landslide. But the media didn't. From the first, the media looked on the Reagan revolution as woebegotten at best. They made war on it. They used their immense influence to blunt it, misreport it, deride it, and to drive key Reagan officials out of office. There was no moment when the successes of the Reagan revolution, or the philosophy under which it operated, was fairly presented in the American press, especially the electronic media. Until the media give up their suffocating liberal bias, they will remain an enemy, and a potent one, of change toward a freer, more morally responsible society.

Still another factor working against reform is the political party. This is not a partisan statement. The Democratic Party did not respond to the Reagan revolution, but then, most of the time the

Republican Party did not respond to it either. Both parties are, after all, in the government business, and they compete to see who can do "more" for us (at our own expense, of course). Never mind if a large majority of Americans want less spending and lower taxes—what do we, the people, have to say about it in the present system?

The House never was under the control of President Reagan. The Senate, even in the period it had a Republican majority, was less controlled by the President than we might have realized. Let me tell you one story about that.

I was President Reagan's appointee, Senate-confirmed, as chairman of something called the National Council on Educational Research. You never heard of it? Congratulations! There are times when I wish I'd never heard of it either. The NCER was set up as a policy-making body to determine the philosophy under which federal research grants in education were allocated. In other words, the NCER staffers are the people who determine today what is going to happen in public schools ten years from now. These people have more of an impact on your life and on the lives of your children than you might think. They gave you, among other things, busing, bilingual education, affirmative action, and the look-say method of teaching how to read, which is the main reason Dick and Jane can run, but cannot read. A whole host of such assumptions had their origins in this little hardcore group of social engineers who decide what the agenda for American education is going to be in the years ahead. The self-serving nature of the educational research community is a well-entrenched bureaucracy in its own right.

President Reagan's agenda—his mandate for educational matters—clearly included the reform of all this. It had four fundamental goals:

1. A return to local community education;
2. More parental responsibility in education;
3. More emphasis on teaching basic skills;
4. Restoration of the teaching of basic values.

Can you imagine any concerned parent in the country who does not approve of all four? Certainly everyone alert to the state of the public schools knows how far we have strayed from basics, and how badly needed these reforms are.

I carried this agenda to Washington, D.C., thinking I was doing exactly what the President wished me to do. But in dealing with the appropriate Senate committee, I found that the then-Republican majority in the Senate was apparently often not in agreement with the President.

Most of our business in those days was conducted with what used to be called the Education and Labor Committee. (They change the names of these committees periodically to protect the guilty; I think this one goes by some other name now.) The committee was chaired by Senator Orrin Hatch, who approved the President's agenda as heartily as I did. Despite the President's overwhelming electoral mandate; despite his educational agenda having the strong support of the American people; despite the Senate committee being chaired by a supporter of the agenda; and despite my own support as chairman of the NCER, we almost always lost. You expect such liberal Democrats as Ted Kennedy and Claiborne Pell to march to a different drummer and to vote against this agenda. But you do not expect Republicans (in the majority, remember) to vote with the liberal Democrats. Senators Lowell Weicker and Bob Stafford, in particular, did so consistently. Just as consistently, those two thwarted the President's efforts at educational reform.

I submit that there is something much more disturbing at work here—namely, the senators themselves are not running things. The Kennedys and Pells and Weickers and Staffords are often not really in charge of their own committees. Frequently, it is their staff people who call the shots. For all practical purposes, it is often the staff people who make the decisions. And so it is that the will of the American people, expressed through the President and through their elected representatives, is frequently thwarted by mere hirelings, elected by no one.

Think about this for just a moment. Think about what is involved in electing one of the one hundred senior legislators for this country, only to have decisions that affect everyone's life made in his name—and often without his knowledge—by his staff. The only authority we, the voters, have granted is to the senator himself.

When his staff can routinely exercise that authority, often in ways that are contrary to the senator's wishes and inimical to the public, our boast of having representative government rings hollow indeed.

Similarly, an unelected bureaucracy rules over many matters in the executive branch. It has a life of its own and is all but uncontrollable. It will not go away no matter whom you send to Washington. Nor can its spots be changed. There is no way a bureaucracy can behave like anything but a bureaucracy. Which means it will always be maddeningly slow, wasteful, boneheaded, anti-social, backward, and awash in rules, forms and red tape.*

The point is, these unelected, faceless staffers and bureaucrats have a horrendous stranglehold on the American body politic, and there won't be any real "revolution" until they go or are reduced *drastically* in number.

Am I implying there really was no Reagan revolution? Or one that was merely a passing fancy with no lasting effect? The media remains in place. The bureaucracy remains in place. The political parties did not change. The nature of government did not change. The federal budget (so-called) mushroomed at its standard ten per-cent per year, compounded. Business was as usual, and one might conclude that nothing happened, or nothing much. But that conclu-sion, I think, would be a serious mistake. There was a Reagan revolution; but it occurred where we wouldn't have expected it. When we understand its real nature, you will see why I remain so optimistic about our future.

Meanwhile, if you were among those who expected a complete overhaul of our political system, your hopes were dashed and you probably have had occasion to recall an older truism: not to put one's faith in the political process. You probably knew that all along, and I think an abiding skepticism about politics is very healthy. Politics is not the way to get things done. I can well understand those who in their enthusiasm for the Reagan mandate

---

*I wrote a short book in 1985, *America by the Throat*, which had all this and much more to say about bureaucracy; with enough examples to make a believer out of even, say, Lenin.

put their skepticism aside for a time. But now we know it does not work. If even a Ronald Reagan landslide can barely dent the system, our hopes of reform lie elsewhere.

Where President Reagan really did succeed was in changing the terms of the debate in this country. Can you recall any time before Mr. Reagan's election that the likes of former Speaker Jim Wright or Senator Kennedy were wringing their hands about the need for a balanced budget? On the contrary, the big spenders then were all saying that deficit spending was *good* for us, that it stimulated the economy. The economy, accordingly, was "stimulated" to its highest Misery Index (the unemployment rate plus the inflation rate) since the depths of the Great Depression. Now the Rostenkowskis and Kennedys are talking about a different way to get their hands on your money: raising taxes to cover the *deficit,* which, of course, is still created by promise-everything legislators spending more than they have to spend. History can guide us here. If the big spenders get their new taxes, they will spend all of that money and more, and we will end up with a bigger deficit. Still, it is a startling improvement that we now find something wrong with deficits in the first place. That change we may properly credit to President Reagan.

Mind, these comments have nothing to do with my feelings about Mr. Reagan in either his successes or his failures. What I am trying to find is the road home. The real point about Ronald Reagan is that he made an amazing breakthrough. He spoke to and for the American people. He spoke to us all from behind the bars and barricades and barbed wire that, figuratively, surround the District of Columbia. He managed to get word out to us from inside the capital Beltway. Everybody (outside) knows that the inside-the-Beltway folks in Washington live different lives, in constant intrigue on how to divide their spoils from taxing 250 million Americans. Mr. Reagan's prime achievement is that he spoke over the heads of the establishment, over the heads of both political parties, over the heads of the media, over the heads of the bureaucracy, over all the intrigues and politicking and weird thinking that marks life inside the beltway. And he did this all the time. He spoke to us, the forgotten folk out here in the country, who just happen to *be* the country. He spoke to us about our own concerns, our real concerns: about the status of our children's education, about our savings for our old age, the regulation of our farms and jobs and businesses, about what was happening in every aspect of our lives. And for the first time, perhaps, in our lives, the American culture, the you and me out there, had an opportunity to speak *our* piece.

The way things have gone since we've had elitist-minded rulers instead of representatives, just to be heard by the powers that be is a revolution. President Reagan spoke of having a strong defense and got our enthusiastic approval. He spoke of the necessity for a vigorous foreign policy, for an effective tax policy that would cut rates to produce more income, for a deregulated economy. In point after point, he spoke to what you and I and most of our countrymen have thought all these years. He sidestepped the whole establishment that has been telling all of us what to do for decades. These establishment types probably couldn't change a spark plug, but they are very sure they know how to run the world. Finally, we had somebody who heard us and talked back to us, despite every effort by the establishment to shut him up.

This is almost always how successful revolutions work. It is rare that we send a person off to political office who then rallies the country in the right direction. Almost always, the rally has already occurred in the leadership community around the country. A new set of ideas comes on the scene and those ideas create a different cultural climate. They are discussed and accepted by civic and academic and church leaders. The change in politics and economics comes later—after the change in ideas.

Richard Weaver, late of the University of Chicago, was fond of a pregnant phrase that has gone into the language in his name: "Ideas have consequences." He was right. Ideas certainly do have consequences, some of which we can predict. This has already happened in our century in another, dramatic revolution. It occurred first at the level of ideas and only later in its massive political impact.

If we go back to about the year 1900 in this country, we'll find that most Americans were generally satisfied with their lives, well-being and work. They lived in a decentralized social order under traditional ideas of limited government, liberty, a strong family, Judeo-Christian moral teachings and personal responsibility. Most were well pleased with the results. But in the same period, a small number of intellectuals were becoming fundamentally discontented with the American way of life. This was something new in our history; never before had there been a truly radical break with America's founding ideas. And at first it might have seemed inconsequential. There were but a handful of radical thinkers, with no wide public following, mostly just writing books and articles for one another. What they discussed so fervently was a wholly different kind of society, essentially a European socialist model. It was to be far more collective, far less individual, far more regulated and planned. This was a vision of the future that was to come to this country.

Who were these people? John Dewey, Charles Beard, Thorsten Veblen, John R. Commons and Richard Ely come at once to mind, and we could add forty or fifty more names with a little digging. All of them wrote in the early part of this century. All of them looked critically at the American past, regarding it as insufficiently collective, controlled and planned. All of them advocated a revolution of ideas to unmake the old America and build a new socialist state. We know with hindsight how effective they were. But nobody would have guessed that at the time. The radicals had no popular following. They could not have won a single congressional race anywhere in the country. All they had was a dream. Yet as their writings circulated, their ideas were discussed and sometimes accepted by other intellectuals and professors. When you begin to influence the professors, what happens? Who comes into their classes? The answer is, the disseminators of ideas: public schoolteachers, clergymen, writers, publishers, other scholars. Within about thirty years, radical ideas had been spread far and wide, and the revolutionary process was complete. What had begun with no public support at all in 1900 had an enormous popular following by the 1930s. It had its political impact in the election of Franklin D. Roosevelt and the imposition of the New Deal, which changed our form of government. Ideas have consequences. It's just about that simple.

Whether this far-reaching change was for good or ill is beside the point. What is important is that a revolution in ideas took place in thirty years, and with such force that this set of ideas has completely dominated American politics in the half century since. When we look at our history in its broad sweep, we easily see the vast changes in our lives and how they grew out of the thought of a few men. This set of ideas only began to crack in any serious way with the election of Ronald Reagan in 1980.

To be sure, some cracks in the collectivist idea had appeared earlier, as witness the phenomenon of Barry Goldwater in 1964. The uncritical will remember that race as a major defeat, Johnson trouncing Goldwater. But the astonishing thing about the race was that an avowed conservative could gain the presidential nomination of a major party. This was the first triumph for a different, anti-collectivist set of ideas. One striking feature of the campaign was a televised speech by a man in a white suit presenting the new ideas: Ronald Reagan, of course. This led to his election and reelection as governor of California, and, in time, to the presidency. Such is the way ideas gradually take hold in our lives.

I doubt that the majority of voters who elected Mr. Reagan in 1980 had any clear agenda in mind. Theirs was a vote against, not a vote for. People knew they didn't want more taxes. They didn't want bigger government. They didn't want more regulation. They didn't want more of the same collectivist fare that they had been force-fed for so many years. As the saying goes, in doubt is the beginning of wisdom. At some point you begin to say, "This isn't right! It has to stop. Enough!" Underlying this feeling are precisely those anti-collectivist ideas worked out and spread in previous years, first by libertarian intellectuals, then by such politicians as Goldwater and Reagan. Whether they could articulate these ideas or not, the American people were serving notice that a cultural revolution was arriving. They would go no further down the old collectivist road. From that day forward, we said, we would take a new direction, toward our traditional ideas and a restoration of freedom and moral values.

We have thrashed all this out in public in the years since, and I think in doing so we have set the terms of the debate for the rest of this century. We began with profound doubt about the way we had been doing things for fifty years. The resultant debate will shape our lives and our children's lives into the century to come. We are all part of the debate. Like it or not, we are all involved. That is the issue we face now. What kind of life do we want in America's future? It is this question and our awareness of its importance that form the principal legacy of Ronald Reagan.

It is this battle of ideas that so concerns us at Hillsdale College. We believe, and we unabashedly teach, that there is a solid case for a prosperous, freely working, open economic system. We need a strong private sector. At Hillsdale, we say it is legitimate to believe in ourselves as individuals, as a people, and as a nation; that it is legitimate to turn again to our American roots and ideals. The odd thing about Hillsdale's role in this debate is that we, too, are a product of the times. We found our own thought responding to the force of cogent new ideas. And we were in the right place at the right moment to popularize these new ideas at the level of public policy—because this was the public policy Americans were ready to accept. As I've related, we were threatened with the loss of our freedom by the federal assertion that we were publicly funded—and therefore subject to regulation—merely because some of our students received federal aid. We had to fight for our independence. That fight began back in 1975 and went all the way to the Supreme Court over a period of ten years. This proved to be exactly the right moment for such an issue to be aired and discussed and debated in this country. A great many people first came to know about Hillsdale at that time.

Among those who came to know us were people in the federal government. I gather they didn't much care for us. A reporter once asked a lawyer at the then-Department of Health, Education, and Welfare—the agency that was trying to stifle Hillsdale—if she knew me. "Yes, I know him," she replied. "And his name is pronounced 'Roche', like the insect."

Of such debate is the future shaped. For many thoughtful people, Hillsdale became a symbol of what you can accomplish privately. Hillsdale proved that you can stay out of the government's clutches and still do something, and do it very well. What we had to do to survive was replace the federal loans and grants our students received. We did it by starting the Freedom Fund, and by approaching people across the country who share our view that a truly private education was both possible and desirable. The generosity and farsightedness of many is helping to guarantee Hillsdale's independence while providing the financial aid for our students that makes it possible for them to attend. We have used not only that money but our reputation for independence in an interesting way. We have been hiring a truly excellent faculty and expanding our curriculum in both scope and quality. Our scholarship funds attract outstanding young people from all over the country; we are attracting excellent students. We have, in short, built a fine educational institution entirely with private funds. This is now recognized in the most unexpected places. Every year *U.S. News & World Report* polls college presidents as to which they regard as the best colleges. I am allowed only one vote, so I can't be accused of ballot stuffing. Every year Hillsdale is listed as one of the better small liberal arts colleges in the country. Similarly, the *New York Times* review of quality schools also recognizes Hillsdale as one of the two hundred best in the country. All this—and with no government money.

At tiny Hillsdale we have become a symbol of independence. We have proved time and time again that it is possible not only to stand for something, but to build a very effective educational institution while taking a stand. In our efforts we have learned that there are people throughout America who are delighted to know that such a school actually exists, and delighted that an institution with courage and purpose and intelligence could be teaching and saying the things they themselves feel. In recognition of this kinship of ideas, we started an innovative seminar series, originally for students and faculty, called the Center for Constructive Alternatives. Over the years more than seven hundred major international figures—Nobel laureates, politicians, artists, theologians, scientists, historians— have come to Hillsdale to speak to our students. The program grew to be such a success that we decided to publish these addresses in a small monthly publication called *Imprimis,* which means "in the first place." I sent the first issue to a thousand friends, hoping some would be interested. Today that list has grown to over a quarter of a million readers worldwide; in the next half-decade, it is expected to double. The success of *Imprimis*, in turn, led to the founding of a special public policy forum which would, in effect, take our highly successful Center for Constructive Alternatives seminars "on the road" for a diverse group of business and community leaders around the country. When it was established in 1981–82, it was called the Shavano Institute for National Leadership. There is a perfectly objective reason for this name: I grew up at the foot of Mount Shavano in Colorado.

All of these efforts over the last eighteen years or so—CCA, *Imprimis*, Shavano—have produced a surprising result: a national Hillsdale audience; indeed, a national Hillsdale *community*. It is a community of ideas, and I meet its members, hundreds of them at a time, wherever I speak around this country, whether it be to a home educators' association in Alaska or a corporate board in New York City.

The point of all this is that it can be done, and done with private funding. What makes it possible is that there are people across America, leaders in their areas, who share these ideas, who feel strongly about them, who are prepared to do something to make them come true, and who are simply delighted to find a frame of reference in which these ideas can be discussed and advanced.

Hillsdale's own story proves that ideas have consequences. What is the consequence of *that* idea for us? If the historical analysis I have presented is correct, then we are at a turning point. The American people have served notice that the old collectivist system is again open to debate. It will no longer be taken for granted. We have said we do not want more of what we've had the last fifty years and are ready for something new. What this means is that we have entered a time of dialogue and discussion. The consensus that emerges from our leadership communities between now and the year 2000 will determine the fate and shape of America in the coming century. You and I live in interesting times at least, perilous times at worst, depending on how we rise to the challenge.

So we see, ideas do make a difference. The real importance of the Reagan revolution does not involve specific policies that succeeded or failed. It should be viewed as a transition point in our culture: one in which old ideas were seriously questioned for the first time, and new ideas were brought forward and given their first hearing. Rethinking who we are and where we are going will set the compass for our children's road. I believe America's leaders have an obligation to join in the process and would imperil the younger generation if they fail to meet their responsibility.

The world can't do much to me, or to anyone who is a little further along in life. What I mean is, it could kill me or take away my property, but it can't change who and what I am as a person. I've been around long enough to be what I am and know what I am, and I imagine this is true for a good many of my readers. As C. S. Lewis said, you can't be a good egg forever: sooner or later you have to hatch or rot. Most of us have been around the block enough times so that we've either hatched or rotted. It's hard to live with sometimes, but it is the way things are for us. We've had a chance to marry or not, to choose a job or business or profession, to live in one part of the land or another, to pursue our religion as we saw fit, to stand up and say what we thought needed saying. We have lived in a country that made all this possible. We were the inheritors of a system and a tradition of freedom fashioned by those before us. In our own times, our traditions and freedoms have been chipped away, one piece after another. Yet enough liberty remains to us so that we have as much freedom as anyone in the world. In many another country, the things I have been saying in these pages would get me lined up against the wall and shot. It is our business and our duty to preserve and expand this freedom for those who follow.

You and I still have the freedom to speak. We and the whole leadership community in America control great resources, moral and intellectual as well as physical. We are guided by a long tradition of what free men and women can do if they choose to. If we do not fight for our freedom and win, who will? We have the best reason in the world to do it: our children. Have you thought seriously about what will happen to them if we fail in our responsibilities? If we don't use the full resources we have to put things right?

The legacy of Ronald Reagan is that once-closed questions have been reopened and our future is once again in our hands. In the next decade, you and I and community leaders on the local school boards or church vestries or business councils will be deciding the direction of America. We will determine its guiding ideas, either by our positive effort or by default. After we're gone, our children will either live in the freedom and dignity and prosperity that we have preserved, or they will live without freedom and dignity and prosperity because we have failed. Let us all be worthy of our task.

Chapter IV

TROUBLE BEGINS AT HOME

Nothing reveals the radical assault on our values as clearly as the decline of the family. I'm sorry to say the government often joins in this assault, in a horribly misguided attempt at paternalism. The results are too often written in human misery.

In the following, keep in mind two principles. The first is basic economics: demand evokes supply; or in shirt-sleeve English, you get what you pay for. The second is almost a mirror image of the first: if you want less of something, tax it. That of course raises the price and reduces demand, also basic economics.

Both of these are obvious tools for government manipulation. We are going to see how manipulative both can be when used for setting "social" policy. Sadly, we will see how destructive they can be when used for *bad* social policy.

One other thing to keep in mind is that the language of alleged social reforms is deceiving. The way to see through it—and here is a technique that is endlessly useful in understanding politics and a lot of other things—is to translate a proposal into its basic economic terms. Specifically, who is getting paid for what and on what conditions? Never mind the wording. Look past that. What are we unhappy taxpayers buying? What we pay for, *we get*.

For a simple example, take "unemployment compensation" or "unemployment relief." It sounds great, and maybe it is a good thing. But before you decide, throw out the wording and instead look at the economics. What are we paying for? Unemployment. And that is exactly what we will get. So long as it pays workers sufficiently not to work, they will not work. In this case we all suffer. We lose the productivity of idled workers. And we who do work have to foot the bill for those who do not, so we have to surrender some of our own life and hopes.

I go through this exercise to alert you that today we are paying for promiscuity, illegitimacy, abortion and broken homes. In fact, we are paying staggering amounts for all of them, and we are getting all we pay for. Indirectly, in the process, we are buying criminality, drugs, gross mistreatment of women, venereal disease, fast-lane homosexuality, the economic, psychological and social abuse of children, a decline in public health and even shortened life spans for many, and bad education.

Repeat: We are buying all this with hard cash. We pay girls to have bastard children. We pay for men to abandon their wives and live the street life. We *tax* to destroy marriage. This is official U.S. Government social policy, all of it. Naturally all of it comes with soothing, "compassionate" labels. But whatever we offer money to "relieve," we buy. Whatever we tax, we reduce. Always ask the economic questions underneath and look at what you are really paying for. Always look at the results.

What we are going to examine is the full-fledged assault on bedrock America. On our homes and families. On the things that matter most, to most of us. This is an attack by radicals who use the power of the media and of coercive government measures to advance their utopian ideals. It may be that many of them mean well, but their ideas are shallow and their handiwork is grim. Utopias have never worked and never will, for they are ignorant of human nature, and in their ignorance, try to make us what we cannot ever be. Here we will see some results of this effort.

Home Sweet Home—Remember?

I believe the family is basic. Until recent decades, almost everybody did. As recently as the mid-1960s, the family was the very core of

American life. It always had been, and we took it for granted that it always would be. Its role was so firm and far-reaching that we hardly noticed its importance. Even less did we suspect that family life could crumble.

But the dreamers and would-be builders of socialism were well aware that families were the enemy. Family life is a rock in the vital process of passing our values and religious beliefs to our children. Without these core values, universally shared, there can be no such thing as civilized society. America as we know it could not exist without our general agreement about what is right and what is wrong. We learn right from wrong almost from the day we are born—if we have a caring family to teach and protect us. The process of handing down our values from generation to generation especially concerns me, as a teacher. It is a primary task of education to reinforce the values first taught at home. But what if there is no home? And what if the teaching of values is banned in our schools?

As we will see, every vestige of religious teaching has been expunged from our public schools. Supposedly "value-free" education—a contradiction in terms—is now the rule. Of course, this just teaches the wrong values.

The radicals have done their work only too well. Today the brunt of their assault falls on home and family. They know that the family must be destroyed before their "utopias" can be built. Their "vision," if so ugly a goal can be called that, fed by radical feminist fantasies, now tends toward a wholly atomized "society" of supposedly free individuals. No sacred or eternal bonds between us will be permitted. We will all be free to flit from flower to flower. We will all be alone. And we will all kneel before the Almighty State, dependent servants of our great master.

Breaking the bond between husband and wife and between parent and child has been the centerfold in most of the utopian schemes that have been put before us. Children will be taken from their mother, or even created by scientific methods in jars instead of wombs, to be taught to serve the omnipotent state.

Those who worship Caesar attack the family by trying to turn our belief upside-down. Remember the slogans of Big Brother in

1984: "War is Peace, Freedom is Slavery, Ignorance is Strength."
What do Caesar's servants say? Among many other things, they say
that marriage is bondage for the wife, so divorce is not only legitimate but a sort of liberation. From this we got "no-fault" divorce
and the repeal of alimony laws. Where once divorce was taboo, we
now have government encouraging it and often paying for it in the
form of "legal aid." One out of two marriages today ends in divorce.
Some experts think two out of three new marriages will fail. Those
thus "liberated," if they manage to remarry, will have a much harder
time in their second, third and fourth marriages. The divorce rate
jumps every step. Divorced women frequently suffer a drastic reduction in their standard of living. Divorced men are prone to every
sort of physical and psychological disorder. The children of a broken marriage, especially if they are young, have a terrible time
adjusting, and are almost always set back in their education. We
will discuss the facts and figures in detail in a later section.

Caesar's servants tell us that sex is just nature's way of saying
"hi," that fornication is fine, and that we ought to shed our inhibitions and behave like bunnies. From this we got the so-called sexual
revolution and hardcore porn in every whistle-stop in America. We
got broken homes and shattered lives. We got a concept of women
as sex objects, as feminists rightly complain, though they seem to
have no concept of how it happened. Women are no longer safe
walking the streets or at times even in their own homes. We suffer
serial killers like the unlamented Ted Bundy, who fuel their lusts
with pornography and then rape and murder our daughters. No
greater oppression of women has ever been devised than to tell them
that moral law is obsolete and that they are free to be promiscuous.
Such "liberation" is a joke on "liberated" women by rich and powerful men. But it turns out the joke is also on other men, and on
civilized society. It is decidedly unfunny.

Abortion vs. Family

Servants of the state tell us that life itself does not matter, that a
woman's "reproductive rights" (code words for the aborting at her

convenience) are precious, and that she may kill inconvenient off-spring through abortion. For all I know, she has a right to eat her young, as some species do at times. This gave us the grotesque *Roe* v. *Wade* decision in 1973 and approximately 1,600,000 dead babies every year now. Do you remember when pregnancy was a "blessed event?" Think hard. All of us believed this once, and not so long ago. Nowadays the burdens of being a mother or father are said to be terrible, and there is nothing blessed about an "unwanted" child. Kill it! But what greater affront can there be to the sacredness of life and the continuity of our families than aborting the next generation?

Honestly, I do not know how a mother could kill her own baby. The bond between a mother and her child is the strongest humans know; a baby at its mother's breast is the very symbol of the sanctity and continuity of life. I do know how the pro-abortion-ists broke this sacred bond: they said the baby in the womb wasn't a baby. They said it was merely a lump of protoplasm—meaningless tissue, not viable life—a possible inconvenience to the mother, and a worthless thing. They also said, incorrectly, that it was part of her body, over which a woman must of course have "control." Do I exaggerate? No, I understate the case. Here is the pro-death view, expressed by a famous and popular advice-to-the-lovelorn colum-nist, in response to a beautiful letter on the joys of life:

> True, an unborn child will never experience any of the wonderful things you described. But neither will an unborn child feel the pain of poverty. Or prejudice. A Hiroshima. A holocaust. Or a nuclear accident. That lucky child will never be terrorized by youth gangs that kill innocent bystanders in random acts of violence. It will never have to fear disease from polluted air or drinking water, or the deadly consequences of playing in a schoolyard unthinkably located precariously near a toxic waste dump.
>
> An unborn child will never be seduced by drugs, or die before he's had a chance to live because of a drunken driver. He will never kill or be killed in a senseless war. (Is there another kind?) And finally, he will never know the pain of being born into a family that doesn't want him, cannot provide for him and resents his presence.

The lady, to be sure, is a geyser of illogic. Does it make sense to kill a baby so that it won't be victimized by dying (Hiroshima, holocaust, toxic waste, drunk drivers, war)? If dying is a bad thing, why does she recommend killing innocent babies? What is more interesting here is that the lady recites the liberal scripture on what is wrong in this world and says that, in the face of all this, you are LUCKY not to live at all. That's her word: "lucky." This is the liberal death wish, put about as plainly as it can be put. Why the lady doesn't do herself in, I cannot imagine. It is runaway hypocrisy. Just possibly she doesn't because she is enjoying an enormous income from peddling this tripe and is glad that she herself was not aborted and spared all the horrors she talks about. Does she spread moral lies for big money? I leave that to you.

Abortion, all but unthinkable until recent years, has now been socially sanctioned by voices like these. Ideas do have consequences, even if they are bad ideas. An equal problem is that abortion is encouraged and sometimes financed by the government, which has acted on the same bad ideas. Tax money flows freely to "do-good" groups that advocate and counsel abortion, though you and I, who pay the taxes, disagree. In this case, conscientious objection is not permitted. Tax law has been rewritten to burden families with children, which makes abortion seem more attractive. *Roe* v. *Wade*, a blatant effort by the judiciary to legislate, and this in response to demands by blatantly feminist, anti-family lobbying, created the most liberal abortion law in the world. Without any constitutional basis whatever, it overturned the laws of all fifty states. It left us with virtually no restrictions on abortion. It is legal to kill a full-term baby. It is even legal to kill the baby if it is born alive after nine months in the womb. And it has been done.

Recent Supreme Court decisions make it clear that the battle over abortion is far from over. It will go on until the American people decide whether or not they condone the taking of human life.

I conclude this sad discussion with a memorable report by *National Review* senior editor Joseph Sobran. Anti-abortionists had been taking garbage bags out of dumpsters at abortion mills, and finding dead foetuses in them. Sobran, "feeling queasy," agreed to be a witness at one night's proceedings.

ChristiAnne Collins showed me what they'd found in dumpsters on previous occasions: tiny mangled human bodies, along with the medical records of the mothers. The abortionists throw all that into garbage bags, so [this group] has to pick it out of the mass of bloody surgical napkins, cigarette butts and empty Coke cans.

ChristiAnne laid out eight of the little bodies on a table. She has preserved these. They are colorless, drained of blood, smelling of formaldehyde. They were aborted at about 10 to 20 weeks after their conception. Some are two inches long, some eight inches, and might have been longer if they had heads. The abortionist usually has to crush the head to pull the body through the mother's undilated cervix.

One of the smaller ones still has a part of her face. Her tongue, a small white tab, is hanging out, and her eyes bulge. The longest one is headless, though ChristiAnne laid a piece of his skull, part of his brain and one of his eyeballs beside him. (The eyeballs often fall out when the head is crushed.)

The lower half of his body is pretty much intact. From the waist up there is only the naked spinal cord plus the right shoulder, arm and hand. His legs are spread apart, with the knees bent and pointing away from each other. At first glance they look like frog's legs until you notice his genitals, his calf muscles and his feet. His toes are curled tensely upward, as if he died in the middle of a spasm.

You can see a few of his internal organs at the point where the upper part of his body has been torn away. If you were dissecting a frog, you'd do it with more care than this little guy got. If nothing else, you'd respect the intricacy of it.

You don't need a theologian to tell you what you're seeing when you look at these. Whoever did it had to know what he was killing. ChristiAnne says an abortionist usually gets close to $2,000 for doing one this far along, as opposed to the usual rate of about $170.

There is more, including a pro-abortion spokeswoman's "suspicion" afterward that the bodies had been "planted," and her charge that anti-abortionists would "stop at nothing." But where would they get dead babies and medical records to "plant" among the other . . . garbage? I feel queasy, too, even thinking about anything like this. But this I can say with perfect certainty: it is the abortionists who will "stop at nothing." I can't help pitying the badly misguided mothers who have killed their own children, not knowing what they do. Only later, too late, will they realize the truth. It will be painful to them, for there could hardly be a woman who does not mourn a lost child all of her days. Later in life, when they should know the joys of having grandchildren to coo over and spoil, there will be emptiness.

Legal Bias Against the Family

Another unexpected but very harmful attack on families is simply over-taxation. The federal tax burden is so high that wives are often forced to go to work, and young families are forced to delay or forego having children. Relatedly, many young people have chosen not to marry to avoid tax penalties. Social scientist and economist George Gilder notes, "Since 1960, all increases in personal taxation have fallen on married couples with children, whose taxes have risen by between 100% and 400% depending on the number of offspring" (in constant dollars). Moreover, the federal tax rate structure has been deliberately manipulated to work against the family. Writes family expert Allan Carlson, "The federal tax burden . . . shifted sharply between 1960 and 1984, as inflation eroded the real value of personal exemptions and the payroll tax soared. For the first time in U.S. history, governmental manipulation of labor markets and income both have a decided anti-child, anti-family bias."

The "manipulation" Carlson refers to began back in the salad days of socialism, near the turn of the century. It was devised by the Fabian socialists in England, the Progressive Movement here, and like-minded groups. Back then, at least the idea was to *defend* the family with such measures as a "family wage" for men and discriminatory wages and restrictions for working women and children, to keep them at home. All of this was engineered by legislation. For instance, there were minimum wage laws for women, designed precisely to discourage their entry into the labor markets (and you thought minimum wage laws exist to protect workers?). None of these measures worked very well. For example, setting women's pay levels lower than men's increased demand for lower-cost female labor, as you would expect. But they did work after a fashion, reaching a high water mark in the 1945–1965 period. Alas, the principle of government intervention in labor markets had been established. It is still very much with us. The difference today is that policy, dictated by feminist and liberal ideas, has done a total about-face and is against the family. The "family wage" of old is illegal. Tax and labor law encourage single life. "Progressives" in Sweden (always on the cutting edge) decided that motherhood was a wasted labor resource, so devised arguments and legislation to shame and force women out of their homes and into the work force—an infection we caught. Young women are "liberated" to join the rat race instead of marrying and having children. This is nothing more or less than official, federal discrimination against motherhood.

The child-care legislation now being proposed is a related attack on the family. Although it is billed as relief for the working mother, it is really an incentive for the mother to go to work in the first place, or to stay out of her home. It is also one more blow to the mother-child bond, taking both out of the home, and depriving the child of at least some of its mother's care and time. Even the best child-care centers are unable to provide the level of care and love that a mother does. Says Gilder, "There is no way governments can replace mothers, no way on earth. There aren't enough re- sources in the world to pay people to lavish on children the kind of care that mothers give in intact families." If the government was concerned about the real welfare of mothers, it could ease their burdens with much higher tax exemptions for dependent children and with tax credits.

It's a free country. I support without reservation the right of any woman to make what she will of her life. But it really ought to be said that there is a serious price to be paid for bad choices, and that ideological propaganda can lead one to bad choices. I do not think that marriage, motherhood, and the nurturing of children in the home—a choice so despised in some feminist literature—is in any way a bad thing or despicable. To the contrary, it is for many a woman a life of fulfillment and ultimate purpose. Their rights to do it should not be denied or derided. It is more. This—not the singles' life and all the promiscuity, the postponing or avoidance of childbearing and all the rest of it—is for many life itself. It is the procreation of our posterity. It is giving our children, and their children and theirs, the moral lessons of life. Nobody does this better than a happily married mother.

The Legal Bias at its Worst

Perhaps the greatest attack of all on the family is federal welfare. In essence, the government pays unthinkable billions of dollars to destroy family life. It pays women to be promiscuous, to have illegitimate children, and to kick the man out of the house. Especially if they are young. Let me again quote George Gilder: " . . . any girl is offered an irresistible solution by the U.S. government. It presents her, at age 16, a chance for independence in an apartment of her own; free housing, medicine, legal assistance, and a combination of payments and food stamps worth several hundred dollars a month. It is a package far beyond the earning capacity of any of her male acquaintances and it is offered without any requirement of work. There is only one crucial condition. She must bear an illegitimate child."

Federal funds for all this "compassion" have increased by a factor of more than thirty in twenty years, since the "War on Poverty" was launched. (Ironically, this is far and away the largest share of the new taxes that are wrecking family life, as we just discussed.) Poverty remains unconquered. What we have mainly done is inflict it on single women and their children, even as government policy encourages them to be single and have children. In general terms, the worst poverty problem we have in this country is the female-headed household.

Bad policy does not discriminate by race; the statistics show that whites are as easily afflicted as minorities. Yet there is no doubt that this disaster falls most heavily on minorities, blacks in particular. Only two black births out of five are legitimate, and among young black women (under age 20) the illegitimacy rate is 90 percent. But note that the rate is no higher in intact, middle-class black families than for equivalent white families. Illegitimacy is very much a problem of the poor, trapped by welfare and living in the inner cities. The rate for all black women in inner cities is often 80 percent or more. These women are usually not loose or immoral in any conventional sense. Rather, they are taking the best economic offer they can get: the government's offer to take care of them in a welfare program. They end up almost literally married to the state, and trapped in poverty. Twenty years of welfarism have effectively overturned moral values. Once taboo, pregnancy is now regarded as the "in" thing, a sort of rite of passage for both the boy and the girl. At one big high school (largely black and Hispanic) in Los Angeles, one girl in four gets pregnant in a given year, and no few of them do it while still in junior high. Marriage does not enter the equation, of course. The state will provide.

The men thus displaced from normal family life head for the streets and a life of rage and frustration, drugs and crime, unemployment and futility. It is welfare that has given us the term inner city, and turned neighborhoods into jungles.

The Bitter Fruit

An incident. A male college student, upon being unable to enroll in a business course he wanted, took a course in women's studies instead. His mother, he said, had been a "bra burner on the campus" in the 1960s, and he thought he might learn something about feminism. What he actually learned was that the male of the species was deemed the Great Satan in these circles, and that no dissent from this view was permitted. "From the first day, they started in about how all men are wife-beaters and child-molesters and how the traditional family, with a mom and a dad, doesn't work," he said. When he ventured to object, he was called a racist and a sexist and thrown out of class. I expect he got a lousy grade out of it too, because the teachers of such dogmas are selling their political wares, not academics, and they often grade according to politics.

Does the "traditional family" work, or are the feminists engaged in propaganda (or worse)? This is a question that can be tested, and in fact has been tested thousands of times in all aspects of family life. Forgive me for generalizing, but I am going to cite the results of hundreds of scientific studies, without pausing to go into too much detail.

Compared to single-parent households or cohabitation without the benefit of clergy: Married couples live longer. They smoke less. They drink less. They "do drugs" less. They spend less time in hospitals. They laugh more, which has therapeutic value proven even in serious disease. They have less serious illness, including some kinds of cancer. They are less prone to cynicism and mistrust, which are linked to early death. They pray more, which has been shown to be helpful in some medical treatments, also including cancer. They are less prone to be angry (a sin in the Christian view), and anger has now been shown to be literally toxic. They have fewer car accidents and pay less in insurance. They think themselves happier. Financially, they are much better off. Their children have much lower infant mortality, suffer fewer deformities and handicaps, are physically healthier, morally healthier, better adjusted, better educated, are better able to think through the long-term consequences of their acts, are more successful by far, and are much less prone to drug abuse, crime, homosexuality, suicide, or life in the streets.

In other words, "old-fashioned" marriage and what we now have to call the "intact" family win hands down in every facet of health and life.

Conversely, men involved in nonmarital households (boy friends or cohabitors) are five times more likely than married men to beat the women and far more likely to abandon them; they are more likely to abuse, injure, kill or sexually molest the children. (The women also beat the men and abuse their children far more often than married mothers.) Cohabiting women are more likely than married women to support the man. The men often make it a virtue not to work and not to support their children; one reportedly impregnated forty-five different welfare mothers. Couples who marry after living together are one-third more likely to divorce, and find marriage less satisfying than couples who did not cohabit first. One in five children in cohabiting homes grows up in poverty. Family income drops one-third after divorce; little of the lost income is recouped within ten years. (Fathers in the intact families had a much better working record.) Much worse, the children suffer a host of psychological problems from which they may never recover. One child in eleven is subjected to drugs before leaving the womb, leading to prenatal drug addiction or to fetal alcohol syndrome, with permanent disabilities. Many such babies have been born with AIDS. (In contrast, parents in a traditional marriage and their children, at least those fortunate enough never to need a blood transfusion, have a zero AIDS rate.)

One other related factor must be mentioned. The rate of violent crime by women is at an all-time high and has been increasing twice as fast as the rate for men. The arrest rate for violent crimes by teenage girls is rising as opposed to a falling rate for boys. Arrest rates for property crimes are similar. The female prison population rose 157 percent between 1978 and 1989. That is more than two-and-a-half times as many women behind bars. Studies indicate that very few of these girls and women are victims of battering and abuse. They are, however, almost always from poor, broken and single-parent homes, rootless homes, and often feel estranged from their families.

The liberal and feminist assault on the traditional family has created what is only just beginning to be recognized as the greatest catastrophe of all: the fatherless home. Apart from all its economic woes, the female-headed, single-parent household is, at least statistically, unable to turn boys into responsible men. The boys born into these homes are being cheated out of their manhood. I know that there are glowing exceptions to this, but too often it is true. Female heads of households themselves often complain that they are unable to control their adolescent boys, and are sometimes abused by them.

I sympathize with the mothers, but that is the least of it. The boys themselves suffer appalling personal problems, and soon enough take their frustrations out on the world. They have lower IQs and do more poorly in school. They are disobedient and beset by emotional instability. They may suffer "father hunger," with symptoms such as "sleep disturbances . . . [inability to sleep], nightmares, and night terrors. . . . " They are institutionalized with serious mental disorders many times more often than boys from homes with fathers. They have intense trouble with their sexual identity, expressed both in homosexuality and in "macho" posturing, exaggerating their maleness. Lacking a model of responsible fatherly behavior, they do not learn good habits or a work ethic, nor do they develop long-term or moral views of life, nor yet do they find a man's role as protector and provider of a family. They have, needless to say, less respect for women, especially in the welfare culture; and as they grow older they make the streets unsafe and commit most of the rapes. All of these problems grow more intense where divorce is the reason for fatherlessness. (Girls in these homes suffer too, of course, but they seem to weather the storms significantly better than boys.)

What happens to these deeply troubled boys when they are old enough to hit the streets? (And they do, at a very tender age, when they don't have a father's restraint.) They start with the usual vandalism and delinquency of unruly kids. Then they harden into the repeat behavior of street thugs. Young, unmarried men commit the majority of all serious and violent crime, and murder is the leading cause of death among them. Suicide is another big cause of death, especially when the parents have divorced; and a little further along, AIDS. Young males without fathers, though a minority by far, commit most rape and arson, mugging and car theft, violence and extortion. Most members of violent street gangs have no fathers. Others are attracted into such hypermasculine religions as Islam, or model their lives after the most successful men they ever meet: pimps and drug dealers. Still others succumb to the most sickening rebellion of all, Satan worship, which in known recent cases has "celebrated" the torture of animals and children, even human sacrifice and cannibalism. (You can catch some of the impetus for that on MTV, not that I recommend it.)

These boys are *lost*. They remain boys, whatever their age, because they had no fathers to teach them to be men. The problem of fatherless homes is the root cause of drug abuse and the crime wave. For problems like drug abuse, we have mistaken the cause. The beginning turns out to be the fatherless home. Drug problems do not develop out of thin air. They grow out of what is missing in human life due to false ideas of what life is all about. They grow out of crazy theoretical notions of what we are, woman and man alike. Once again, we see how much ideas have consequences. And when we send our young men, morally unarmed, into this world of ideological fantasy, they pay dearly themselves and they turn the streets to jungles. This is common to all races, nations and economic standards, and it is known *not* to be caused by poverty. (Serious crime can be predicted with extraordinary precision by fatherlessness, but the effect of poverty is slightly negative—tending away from crime. So much for liberal theories that poverty causes crime.) Nor is it strictly a welfarist problem, though that is where it is by far the worst.

Federal policies—developed from liberal and feminist delusions—encourage (that is, pay good money for) fatherless homes, in the guise of "helping" unmarried women and their children in hundreds of ways. The government, as we have seen, spends many billions of dollars yearly breaking up homes. It pays girls to get pregnant (so long as they remain unmarried), gives them free apartments, food stamps, cash aid per child, and many other such benefits. It also penalizes, with much heavier taxes, those who manage to marry and form a traditional family. Coming up: tax-paid day care centers, government-mandated maternity leave and flex time, and other incentives to take women out of their homes; as before, an ideological assault on our homes and families.

As a result of this massive assault, barely half (the most recent figure is 52 percent) of all Americans live in families today. That is: the traditional family of father, mother and children. Indeed, we sometimes have to call this a "nuclear family" or an "intact family" to make clear what we mean. So many other arrangements are being tried and called "families" that even the meaning of the real thing is slipping away.

All this shows a dreadful confusion about what a family is and why it is so important to civilized life. In truth, this is a moral question, and radical reformers hate to let moral law get in their way. Or, they say it is all superstitious nonsense from the past. *They* know better. But we can learn from experience, you and I. We can see the results of "reforms" that they force on us by law and can in many cases measure those results with scientifically valid methods. In short, we can, and should, hold the reformers to account for their handiwork. Let's look further at what they have done to the family.

One marriage in two ends in divorce. "Liberalizing" divorce laws, along with arguments that marriage is bondage rather than the deepest human bond, has made divorce fashionable and easy. We even have no-fault marriage ceremonies disposing of such old inconveniences as offering our most sacred vow, before God, to build our marriage till death do us part. If we won't make such a vow to dedicate ourselves to our marriage, it's small wonder that we so often end up in court.

As one consequence, nearly 60 percent of children born today—a significant majority—will not make it to age 18 in a normal family. Somewhere along the line they will end up in a one-parent household. Only two in five will live at home with both of their parents (nowadays we have to say "biological" parents). If nothing else, the unfortunate majority thus start life with considerable economic and social disadvantages. Psychological damage to the children in a broken home tends to be much worse, and it lingers on and on. You can imagine as well as I what a terrible experience it is for children to hear their parents raging at each other, to feel unloved, to feel dread and fear and guilt that they are the cause, and have their secure life and home torn apart. Afterwards, chances are high that they will be moving to a new residence. Nobody can adjust to this sort of battering, but it is much the worst for children, and it scars them deeply. According to a major study—the findings of which surprised its author—"It would be hard to find any other group of children . . . who suffered such a rate of sudden, serious psychological problems." Ten years after the divorce, "41 percent [of them were] doing poorly: they were entering adulthood as worried, underachieving, self-deprecating and sometimes angry young men and women. The rest were strikingly uneven in how they adjusted to the world; it is too soon to say how they will turn out." The children "longed for their fathers and the need increased during adolescence." Mom and Dad weren't doing very well either. Fully a decade after the divorce, a fifth of the fathers and a quarter of the mothers hadn't gotten their lives back in order.

Not surprisingly, children of divorced parents have major problems in education. So do those that emerge from the welfare trap of the inner cities and female-headed homes there—if they don't just drop out of school altogether. These are matters that particularly concern me. We talk about our "education" problem, and we certainly have one. But we should ask, more searchingly than we do now, "why?" Says one acute observer, "The decline in math and science scores, the illiteracy problem, homelessness and greatly diminished income for women can all be linked to the higher divorce rate." That is the sort of thing we confirm with statistics, but it makes sense on any terms. The well-reared, morally instructed child from a stable, loving home is simply going to do better in school. To such as these, the world is a good place and they are eager to learn about it. But children who have had the cruel experience of divorce or an unfulfilled home life do not want to learn. And who can blame them?

Another study, another closely related statistic. Children who do not get a full measure of tender, loving care at home can easily turn out to be "psychopaths." Here, the term is general, and does not imply that they are necessarily going to go out and empty their Soviet AK47 assault rifle in the schoolyard. But it might indeed turn out that way, along with certain other "high risk" lives like "slick salesmen" or—I kid you not, this was in the study—politicians. And, yes, sadists, serial killers and all other horrors of our times. The case was that children without enough love or "bonding" to their parents could grow up without a conscience. The greater their lack of loving care, the less conscience they might have. Interesting! I could quibble with the cause of this—perhaps lack of love is confused with lack of moral teaching? But the two are so intimately related, there is no doubting the answer. A friend once gave me what I think is the best definition of love: an enduring concern for the *moral* well-being of the beloved. We love our spouses by caring deeply about the enduring commitments of marriage. We love our children, not only by hugs and kisses, but by drawing lines and limitations for them: teaching them by word and example what is right and wrong. Love is moral fulfillment.

Returning to that study, what is starkly obvious is that it is the

children of broken or one-parent homes who most suffer this kind
of deprivation. "Kids without conscience," they were called. Is
there anything worse we can do for our children than leave them
without a conscience? And given the circumstances in which this
arises, should we not do everything in our power to refute the false
ideas that promote illegitimacy, promiscuity, abortion, easy divorce
and all the rest of it? We must rebuild the loving, secure, and if I
dare say so, Christian home.

Can you stand more statistics? Let's go back to "poverty."
We Americans do like a comfortable, well-provisioned life. And
we enjoy one absolutely unknown in all the history of earth. A status
below the government's present poverty line still allows many luxuries unknown to the most opulent ruler of ancient times.

Let us be clear here: material comfort certainly is not fulfillment in life. We are instructed not to get too attached to the treas-
ures of this earth. But there is certainly nothing wrong with enjoying
the fruits of our labor. As a historian, I find an extraordinary connection between moral behavior and a prosperous life. Our own
country is the prime example. Here we have enjoyed a freedom
unknown in history, coupled with—or I should say, fostered by—a
deeply religious understanding of life. The result has been an explosion of invention and capital investment that has made us rich. I
think these things are interlocked, without any trace of doubt. We
owe our prosperity to our *goodness*.

Materialists take note: as we stop being good, we are going to
lose it all. And for this, too, the statistics have a story, as well as
our own moral sense. By any measure, a home broken by either
divorce or welfarist promiscuity is on its way downhill—drastically.
The man may come out better in economic terms, after "liberation"
from his duties to his wife and children. The woman rarely does.
According to recent figures, "female-headed" households are about
seven times as likely to sink into poverty as intact families. More
than one female-headed household out of three is below the poverty
line. I am by no means asserting that these women are immoral.
But one can say that a very large number of them have been de-
ceived. Some have been persuaded that bearing illegitimate babies
is just fine and it pays. Some have been persuaded that marriage is

by and large a bad deal. A few, I suppose, are militantly hostile to men in general, along good feminist lines, and see the male of the species as oppressors. But is any of this the way things are? If it is, why do we have all these horrid statistics from experience showing that all of our departures from traditional moral understandings do so much harm?

Crime, psychopathic behavior, psychological battering, drug use, poverty, inner-city devastation, educational failure, street culture and so many other problems can be traced directly to the decline of the old-fashioned family. What more can we possibly know before we rediscover the truth? Our fathers and mothers before us knew the truth. It is we who have failed.

Some Parting Thoughts

We make problems for ourselves. But we never have to. That is the main point here. We can do things the way they work, and if we have forgotten how they work, we can learn again. Let us learn again.

In the Christian conception, men and women are halves, each with its own nature, but not wholly fulfilled until they join into "one flesh." It asks us to give up part of ourselves: to subsume ourselves in the marital union, so that we may find this unique fulfillment. It warns us sternly that the union is permanent and may not be put asunder. Men and women who take seriously their Christian vows of marriage tend to have good and lifelong marriages. Great is their reward.

In the modern, secular conception, men and women are wholes and free to be what they will, virtually without moral restraint. This may seem a tempting idea and a new level of freedom, but it offers no moral basis or direction in marriage. What deep and abiding obligation is there to hold two free people together? What commitment do they make, other than pre-nuptial agreements not to give up too much property upon divorce? But without the commitment and moral essence of marriage, divorce very likely is going to come along one day.

As we have seen, this is enormously problematic, not only in the heartbreak of those involved, but for America. By believing the underpinnings of cohabitation, abortion, easy divorce and the rest of it, we are destroying our own children. Can any graver charge be brought against us?

The evidence is in, and it is overwhelming. The old ways were right, as those of us who heeded moral teaching knew all along. The flaming ideology of those who rant against millennia of human understanding and sympathy can be measured in an epidemic of drug abuse, venereal disease, crime and frustration. Frankly, I doubt that we can do much for the obsessed folks who peddle this stuff. The sooner their breed dies out, as it necessarily will, the better. But you and I can certainly do something for their victims: most of all, children.

Women: What have I to say to you? This only. Don't get conned by theories that motherhood and home and family are low estates for the modern woman. Stand your ground against any and all fads and fashions—and laws—that take away from your nature, your home and home life, your special love of children, and all that you do so well. There is no substitute for your own unique touch. Guard your daughters' moral health, which is the meaning of love. It is not you so much as men who have been hornswoggled by crazy talk in our times. In the so-called sexual revolution, men were the "winners," with easy access to women who have been told by charlatans that they would be fulfilling themselves with casual sex. This is, to say the least, the easy way out for men so morally lazy that they can, and do, abandon responsibility to their temporary "mate" and their children. But it turns them into un-men. This repulsive victory is celebrated with a laugh and the latest centerfold. If women are easy, men are never going to be men. Why should they bother? When you talk about the scarcity of good, eligible men, think twice about the slogans of feminism.

Men: Teach and take care of your own children first. But at the first free moment, think of boys you know who do not have a father. Share time with them whenever you are able. Teach them what it is to shoulder a man's responsibility. Help them learn to respect, take care of and love mother, sister and wife; to provide and protect; to build their home and spiritual strength. Take a fatherless boy under your wing and make him a man. He needs you to give him what he can't get at home. You and I can do this on our own, and we know that we will do more good by it than all the bureaucrats on earth. This is a job only men can do.

Chapter V

CONFUSION IN THE CLASSROOM

Cicero told the unvarnished truth in saying that those who have no knowledge of what has gone before must forever remain children; and if one wished to characterize the collective mind of this present period, or indeed of any period . . . one would do it by the one word *immaturity*.
—Albert Jay Nock, *Memoirs of a Superfluous Man*

If there are two propositions all Americans agree with, they are these. First, the school system is a mess. Second, whatever problem we face, great or small, the solution is more education.

This sounds like more of a contradiction than it really is. More and better education is certainly desirable, if not a cure-all. It is needed precisely because the public schools are not providing it, or are doing it very poorly.

It is not that our young people have been underexposed to "education." In this century, unlike the last, all American children go to school. And they spend vastly more time in class than has been usual in other periods and places.

Rather, it is that they have been badly shortchanged in what they receive from schooling. Youngsters enter the system at age six, and spend the next twelve years there, often sixteen if they go on to college, doing—what? After all this, a startling and sad number of them cannot read, or do arithmetic, or speak in complete sentences, or write a coherent paragraph. Reading and writing are first- or second-grade material, easily taught to any normal child. How is it possible to graduate from high school or even college without knowing the "Three Rs"?

Learning to read is not nearly enough. What students read, and with what critical faculties they appraise it, matters more. In high school and especially in college they will be obliged to read books and hear lectures calculated to undercut traditional values. Will they have the background, training and mental tools to know when they are being sold a bill of goods? If they do, they didn't learn them in school. Yet the foremost duty of education is to transmit America's heritage, beliefs and values from the old generation to the new.

Often, all too often, the young people will be turned out into the world with their smattering of "facts" and "skills," as so much Silly Putty to be shaped by the servants of power. Most can read, but are untrained in logic, rhetoric or argumentation, and so are unable to evaluate what they read. This leaves them defenseless before ideologies and demagogues. They will be lucky to have encountered more than a few of the ideas that have animated Western civilization for two thousand years. They will be much luckier if they have had more than a taste of our great poets and playwrights, artists and composers, philosophers and theologians; or of our history, founders and heroes. Without these things, they cannot know why the West is good, and worth defending. Neither can they recognize our enemies or repel the attacks against us—especially from those America-haters among us who labor to bring down our civilization.

Surely a system that treats our children like so many units off the assembly line; that leaves them at best semi-literate; that tells them little of their history or heritage; that does not teach them systematic thought; that starves them of moral value and the qualities of a whole and human life; in short, that does not educate—this is a system in need of rethinking and major overhaul. We pour unlimited amounts of money into the *mechanics* of education. It is time to think of *what* we teach.

Schools for Socialism

Let me suggest something so plain and obvious it sounds shocking: the public school system is doing exactly what it is intended and designed to do. It is turning out exactly the mass-produced, uneducated, "socialized" product it wants to turn out.

We see it as failing in its task because we assume it is trying to educate our children. But it is not. We mistake its purposes. Its business is to condition them for social change. By its own lights, the system is doing very well.

Lest you think I exaggerate, using the schools for social engineering has been the heart of "educationist" theory* since the turn of this century. The theory not only remains in force, it has grown more and more radical over the years. Nor ought we be surprised that government schools end up serving primarily the purposes of government, rather than those of education or private life. Or more particularly, they serve the purposes of power-wielders in or out of government. Bureaucracies always work in their own self-interest, and the educationist bureaucracy certainly is no exception.

You needn't take my word for it. The educationist elite, the bureaucrats, the teachers unions, are all fairly open about their

---

*Under the influence of the Progressive movement, and in a very short period, the "grand old fortifying curriculum" of education was rooted out and banished. It was "the dead hand of the past," useless in a new, forward-looking America entering the twentieth century. Education was replaced by training, the content of which was virtually dictated single-handedly by John Dewey and his Instrumentalism. The ideas of a fixed reality, natural law and the work ethic were to be expunged. The schools were to be used to breed a new generation of Americans who would prefer group and social actions, and who would regard themselves as individuals no longer, but as members of a "total democratic society." The new American was to be guided by the dictates of social harmony. No individual or moral values were to interfere with that social harmony.

These counter-revolutionary doctrines swiftly pervaded the school system and remain its driving force some eighty years later. In the process, the classical meaning of "education" was discarded by common consent, and thereafter training was called education. One other change is worth noting. When the schools were turned into a tool for social engineering, attendance became compulsory. When you are creating an anthill society, you have to catch all the ants.

efforts for radical "change." They may disguise their language, so as not to arouse resistance by the unsuspecting majority. They may call themselves political "activists" instead of liberals or socialists, and refer to their "movement" for the "cause" without saying what the "cause" is. But there is no doubting the thrust of their thinking and work. We can allow that their intentions are good. They believe that they are serving a grand new vision for mankind as fervently as I believe that they have forgotten what paves the road to hell.

We needn't consider intentions. The results are before us. Whether planned or not, the public school system could hardly serve statist appetites any better than it does. The principal defenses against state usurpations are religious belief, a firm code of civil and moral values, and an understanding of history. These are, or were, precisely the qualities imparted by genuine education. They have all been ruthlessly expunged. History texts have been rewritten so as to "debunk" America's Founders and heroes and to make them look like oppressors. All reference to the role of religion in American life has been removed. Teaching has been made "value-free" so that children do not learn right from wrong. Prayer or any sort of moral instruction is illegal; and lawyers from "civil rights" groups are on duty twenty-four hours a day to sue in case worship breaks out in some backwater school.

Bluntly put, the school system seems designed to *prevent* education, not to offer it. Teacher and student alike have suffered while the educationist bureaucracy has puffed up and prospered. Federal aid has accelerated the whole process, helping to produce an increasingly dangerous situation. Richard Weaver in *Visions of Order* saw it more than a quarter of a century ago, and things have skidded badly since then:

> It is not too much to say that in the past fifty years public education in the United States has been in the hands of revolutionaries. To grasp the nature of their attempted revolution, we need only realize that in the past every educational system has reflected to a great extent the social and political constitution of the society which supported it. This was assumed to be a natural and proper thing, since the young were to be trained to take places in the world that existed around them. They were "indoctrinated" with this world because its laws and relations were those by which they were expected

to order their lives. In the period just mentioned, however, we have witnessed something never before seen in the form of a systematic attempt to
undermine a society's traditions and beliefs through the educational establishment which is usually employed to maintain them. There has been an
extraordinary occurrence, a virtual education coup d'etat carried out by a
specially inclined minority. This minority has been in essence a cabal, with
objectives radically different from those of the state which employed them.
An amazing feature of the situation has been how little they have cared to
conceal these objectives. On more than one occasion they have issued a
virtual call to arms to use publicly created facilities for the purpose of
actualizing a concept of society not espoused by the people. The result has
been an educational system not only intrinsically bad but increasingly at war
with the aims of the community which authorizes it. [Richard M. Weaver,
Visions of Order, pp. 260–261]

We begin to understand what Weaver meant in saying, "all
education is learning to name [things] rightly." If we called public
schooling a "socialized" system, as it undeniably is, we would
expect the socialized product we get. No one would be puzzled that
our children are being stamped into identical little statists-to-be (or
as near to that as the system can get). That is the plan. And if we
questioned the reasons that state schooling is compulsory, we would
see the danger in it much more clearly. What is the reason? To
make sure that all children get an education? That is sheer nonsense.
The fact is, the public schools fail to give to many students an
education worthy of the name. If their purpose is to educate, they
flunk miserably and should be replaced by something that works.
If they serve other, political purposes—a far greater menace—then
they cannot pretend to be educational institutions at all, and ought
to be abolished. It does not matter whether they serve the "right"
politics or the "wrong" politics. You do not inflict political theories
on little children in the name of teaching them.

If there is any "bright" spot in the situation, it is that bureaucracy doesn't work. The school system cannot educate, but neither
can it ultimately effect the radical "change" that the educationists
seek. It cannot make us into something we are not, however shamelessly it uses coercion and indoctrination to try. Human nature is
what it is. Our individuality and spirit cannot be taken from us.

What little success the public school system enjoys is due to decent, skillful teachers who still care about teaching (there are many), and youngsters who want to learn and find ways to do so. Both have to defy state directives and buck the system to get anywhere. But they do it. They are survivors.

I know, because we get some of the best of these young people at Hillsdale College. Somehow, they manage to swim upstream in the public schools, and get something out of the experience. I have met thousands of them in my classes and in other functions of a small college. And I meet their teachers, often in person, or at least as a reflection of what the students know and think. I teach and I know teachers. Yes, there are many wonderful teachers still around. And no, neither they nor their determined students will ever be wholly frustrated in seeking education. But all of us understand their successes are not a product of the system, but the opposite: the result of defeating or defying the system.

And that is the problem. What we all want is education for our children. What most of us must suffer to provide it is a huge, immensely expensive, self-interested bureaucracy. Of what use is a state schooling system that thwarts our hopes and makes young people have to fight to learn anything? This will not do. We are a practical people and know we have to use the right tools to get the job done. Public schools are the wrong tool. They cannot hope to do much better than they do, much less succeed in truly educating, without drastic restructuring to restore local and parental control. I doubt this is possible, and do not think it is the best answer available to us. But before we get to those points, let's see what we are up against now.

Why Public Schooling Must Fail

It is important to realize how long these same questions have been raised. All of us were "born into" the system as it is. Almost all vestiges of the old, "classical" education had disappeared by the year 1900. What replaced it was meant to be modern, scientific, practical training (which has little in common with education, however useful it may be), available to all under the management of government. The old education had its problems and was suited more to the few than the many. That was considered elitist, and was a big strike against it in a democratic setting. It left some, many, children out. But the new style had its problems too. From day one, the whole system sputtered and coughed. The adjustments, tuning, new University Plans, tinkering and reforms that were tried to make it work would fill a bookshelf. We are still trying. But it never did work very well, and it has built-in factors that make it work even worse as time goes on.

Sixty years ago, Albert Jay Nock, a close and interested observer of the changes, noted: "As soon as the system was on its way to becoming a going concern with the taxing-power of the state behind it, the path of least resistance lay open to a rapidly increasing flow of persons whose interest in education was secondary." That is, secondary to making money. True enough, tax-paid jobs, then and now, do not pay as much as high-pressure jobs in private business. But they are unbelievably secure, less demanding, and far better paid than most alternative jobs for persons of limited ambition. In latter days, they have also offered astonishingly generous fringe, retirement and pension benefits, to be paid by present and future taxpayers.

And what (apart from damage to the taxpayers) is wrong with that? Simply this: teaching is and always has been a dedicated profession. You can't do it strictly for money. Much of your compensation is in seeing that you impart knowledge and values to the new generation. You are paid in part by your satisfaction at watching your pupils grow up with what you taught them, and then in teaching their children, and perhaps even their grandchildren too, as James Hilton's Mr. Chips did. Devotion to education is the only thing that makes this happen. Money never will; money is not enough; money isn't the right compensation.

The drudges attracted by our bureaucratic school system and its perks care about their position, their security, their modest but unfailing paycheck. They do not put the demands of education first. And they cannot. They have, as bureaucratic regulations require, passed through the so-called "education" schools at the big universities. There they will learn a little about how to teach and next to nothing about what to teach. Their own SAT scores are near or at the bottom of college entrants. They are, as Boston University President John Silber put it, of borderline educability themselves. And they are supposed to educate?

What really happens is that our pool of teachers sinks lower and lower in its abilities and aspirations, each generation less willing and certainly less able than the last to meet the duties of teaching. As in any bureaucracy, the easy-way-out, cover-your-rear, time-serving people take over. All they have to do to advance is wait it out while the talented people get discouraged and find something else to do. We get some of our best teachers at Hillsdale because they can't stand the bureaucratized, by-the-rules, stultifying atmosphere in state universities, and indeed, in some private colleges and universities. They want to teach. They want to give of themselves. But they can't do it by regulation and by rote. So they come to us at Hillsdale, attracted by the freedom and independence from government that we have defended for almost a century and a half. And we are very glad to have them. They are the right kind of teachers, the only kind any real educational institution would want.

These problems, and many more, all flow from the nature of public schooling as a political rather than a market enterprise. The school system is a monopoly and has all the worst features of a monopoly. It is tax-"funded." You are forced to pay for its services whether you like them or not, or whether you even use them. No business can do that to you. Businesses have to serve you and your wishes, and do it efficiently, or they are gone. In this schooling "market," your needs mean little or nothing, and there is nothing you can do about it. Not only are you forced to pay, but to pay more and more for less and less education as years go by. The bureaucracy's appetite for taxes is limitless, and its ability to waste money is legendary.

School attendance by your children is compulsory. For the large majority, that means taking what the public school monopoly offers or else. The only escape is attending private schools. These in turn are regulated and controlled as much as possible by the same educationist bureaucracy, using such legal tools as licensing, teacher certification, and review of curricula to meet state "standards." It is only a partial escape but it *is* something. They make you pay double for it. First, you have to pay for the state schools with your taxes. Then, if you have any money left for tuition (and boarding and extra transportation), you can send your child to a private school.

Private schools generally cost less, but the extra burden, after school taxes, is too much for most parents. The astonishing thing in recent years is that so many parents have been able to scrimp and sacrifice enough to get their children out of public schools, and to turn private education into a boom. I hate to think what it costs them. But I admire their effort and their reason for it. They recognize that their children are being cheated in public schools, and worse, are being subjected to political or anti-religious doctrines. (Most of the private schools have religious affiliations.) With good reason, they object to "value-free" teaching and the likes. Mandatory sex education, justly described by columnist Cal Thomas as "a form of spiritual and political molestation." Bilingualism. Forced busing. Suppression of religion and denial of religious influence in our history. Graphic and "value-free" "education" about AIDS. (Buggery is unhygienic, kids.) Such are the results when bureaucrats get handed a monopoly in state schooling. Small wonder parents suffer so much hardship in order to get their children out of the system.

And, in keeping with the bureaucratic way of doing things, all schoolchildren must "advance" at the same pace which, of necessity, is the pace of the slowest and dullest among them. The public schools, obliged to take all pupils and treat them equally, are faced with the fact that children are not equal. The only answer to this, in a bureaucracy, is to defy reality and reduce all teaching to the least common denominator. If your child is bright and should learn much more than is taught at the levels set by bureaucrats, too bad for your child. If he or she is bored to desperation by state school pap and turns against learning, there is no remedy. Many do rebel. You won't get anything better, ever, with this system. Under bureaucracy, everything must be geared to the poorest students—not least for the benefit of incompetent teachers.

The system has added some refinements that none of us could

have anticipated. Whatever the course, whatever the results, everybody passes. The theory behind that is, you develop socially according to your age group. Never mind whether you advance academically. Your social development would allegedly be stunted if you got left behind. (There is some truth to this; but the chance of flunking used to be a strong incentive for kids to work hard and keep up. What could be more embarrassing than to be stuck back with the little kids, or, worse, your younger sister or brother?) The immediate result is, it is nearly impossible to flunk a year in any public grade school. It is hard to flunk anything even at the high school level. Knowing this, many students naturally goof off and ignore their studies. They have no incentive to work. The long-term result is some high school and even college graduates who cannot read.

Consumers have no control over a monopoly school system because they are forced to pay, regardless. It is a political machine, and the only thing that can influence it is politics. And politics is innately state-centered. We need not wonder that public school teachers are unionized, that their main union (the National Education Association) is the biggest in the country, and that it is politically active and liberal. (How they dare claim "education" in their name, I cannot imagine.) The NEA consistently opposes teacher pay based on performance or merit. Just as consistently, it insists on bureaucratic pay scales. These are left-handed, but honest, assessments of their own capabilities: The unionists as a rule can't make the grade. Being a part of the bureaucracy pays a lot better and is a lot easier than actually teaching. Case closed. If these good folk were in the teaching business to teach instead of for the money, they would not be drumming bureaucratic pay. Can you imagine Socrates, or Mark Hopkins,* forming a teachers' union?

Unionization is just a symptom of how political the system is.

---

*"[This is] the value of a true teacher. Give me a log hut, with only a simple bench, Mark Hopkins on one end and I on the other, and you may have all the buildings, apparatus, and libraries, without him."—President James A. Garfield. Hopkins (1802–1887) was a prominent educator and president of Williams College.

Politics invites in the dreamers and world-savers and do-gooders. What especially attracts them is the opportunity to impose their radical ideas by brute force. Their audience is literally captive, and they do not hesitate to dictate to it their political nostrums. Exactly the same means thrived in Nazi Germany, dictating to the *Hitler-jugend* (Hitler Youth Group). The radicals' targets are your children, and their power over your children stems from your own money, taxed by the school monopoly. They consider the whole school system their private preserve, and go to any pains to expand their monopoly control and their power to indoctrinate whole generations. Here is just one sample of many, from a recent prize-winning essay for the American Humanist Association: "The battle for humankind's future must be waged and won in the public school classroom by teachers who correctly perceive their roles as *proselytizers of a new faith*" (emphasis added). Those we have in droves. But how do you like teachers and educationists conspiring to destroy your child's faith in God? And by whose lights are the schools a "battleground" for advancing radical ideas? Ever since Dewey's ideas took over three generations ago, children in the public school system have been regarded, and treated, as guinea pigs for use in social engineering. They are for . . . experiments. This is as far from real education as you can get. It is infuriating. But you can't do anything about it within the present system.

You can't, but radicals can. The utopians are acutely aware that public schoolchildren are theirs to molest under the system of bureaucracy, and they find in this a golden opportunity. It is not very hard to do if your views are in harmony with the socializing system, and if you pose as a public interest group doing good for the children. (It is illegal if your views are religious.) Just send your "program," your films and tapes and advisory materials for the teacher; all this will insinuate its way into public teaching.

For many years there have been no end of such programs in the school system, all of them liberal-left. The unilateral disarmers have had programs. The anti-nuke people have programs. The self-proclaimed environmentalists and gay/lesbian activists and peaceniks and animal-rights people contribute to programs. The friends of the Soviet Union would like your child to "understand the Soviet

Union," where folks, after all, are just like us, and none of this foolish talk about state oppression, mass murder, slave labor camps or military aggression. There are programs for a "global" outlook that sing the praises of the Third World, and, curiously, leave the civilized world looking uncivilized in comparison. They didn't listen to P. J. O'Rourke, a visitor to some of the most hellish backwaters on earth, who says: "Civilization is an enormous improvement on the lack thereof. No reasonable person who has had a look at the East Block (or an issue of the *Nation*) can countenance the barbarities of the Left."

None of these, I suspect, is half as destructive as a program for 13 to 15-year-old children called *About your Sexuality*. It is presented, as they all are, with film strips and the like, only in this case the material is sexually explicit in the extreme. There is less left to the imagination than in hardcore pornography. This we could, perhaps, stomach if the purpose was basic instruction in biology and the facts of life and hygiene. But in truth the whole course is an invitation to every imaginable form of sex, with no detail too gamy or perverted to omit. It is unprintable in this book or in any normal or family publication; but in the system, nothing is too perverted to force-feed to prepubescents at their most vulnerable and impressionable age. And of course, no moral distinctions are drawn. There is no right and wrong in this. All is relative. Whatever feels good is dandy. Indeed, it would not be possible to assign any moral values to material like this. If you think your children, repeat, a captive audience, are simply being taught the facts of life, you are badly mistaken. They are being indoctrinated in sexual degeneracy with scarcely a word of warning about the price to be paid for it.

Perhaps the worst factor in all of this is that all the decisions and directives come from above. It is all centralized now. Your local school board has little to say in managing your schools, and you have even less. What will be taught has all been decided already. If you are lucky, you may get on a textbook selection committee and will help to choose between as many as six state-approved texts, each as bad as the next. Your state educationist bureaucracy cannot help you much. It is financed and, therefore, controlled by yet another bureaucratic layer, at the federal level.

The exasperating thing is, every layer of bureaucracy adds immensely to the cost of your child's "education," even as it is making a mess of that education. This, too, is inherent in a monopoly. Costs get jacked up as much as the traffic will bear—most of it for "administration" and overhead. By doing away with the bureaucracy and returning schools to local control, costs could be cut drastically and results improved.

All the negatives we have discussed are inherent in socialized schooling. The system is necessarily monopolistic, centralized, state-serving, bureaucratic, bossy and overexpensive. It is barely able to teach, and can teach no more than the slowest student can grasp. It is political in origin and function, and having the power to indoctrinate, imposes its own political, ever-more-radical theories. Its purpose is not to educate but to defeat education and thereby condition children to its designs.

It will do us no good to tinker with the machine to try to get better results. All these problems flow from the nature of the system. We are using the wrong tool. Malcolm Muggeridge, never one to mince words, says that the whole thing is liberal pishposh, a "gigantic fraud," that is or may as well be intended to bring down civilization. Ponder that. In no other area do we expect a massive, monopolistic bureaucracy to be productive, dedicated and efficient. Why do we allow one in education, the most important area of all? I can't think of one good reason. Perhaps we think it is hopeless to address the real problems because we can't change the system. But that is underestimating ourselves. I think we can do a lot about it (see Chapter VII).

I have one modest question. If state schooling is a good thing, why are we *forced* to pay for it, and why are our children *forced* to attend? That is not the way things are done in a free country, or in any civilized setting. We do not go around forcing our neighbors to buy what we sell at gunpoint. It is a crime. Why is the same act any better when it is the government forcing us to accept its shoddy schools? It isn't. It is the same act of force, for the same purpose.

If the government has something really good to sell in its schools, at the right price, it will have a market. That it forces its output down our throat by taxes and truancy laws is all the proof anyone needs that its compulsory schooling is a scam.

For three generations, our national leaders of both parties and all persuasions have failed us. Their endless promises to "improve education" have given us a miserable school system that just keeps getting worse. If they will not do anything about it, then you and I must.

The only real answer to the questions which bedevil us in public education lies in a market test, allowing parents and communities to sort out their own solutions. As we set about the task of educating our children, what are the fundamental questions, and what answers does market choice offer?

What are these questions? Size, for one. For years I have been warning that the trend toward consolidated, larger schools is a step in the wrong direction. It is true that the larger school can provide more specialization, more counseling, more testing and more gadgetry. But it is also true, and more important, that in such schools the students and teachers start to lose that personal contact that is the essence of education. Teaching is very personal: Mark Hopkins on one end of the log, the student on the other. In the large, bureaucratized facility, with all its professionalized sports and activities and layers of administration, teaching turns into an assembly line. There is little room for teacher-student contact. I am not arguing for a return to the little red schoolhouse (well, I could, and with Adam Smith as my witness), but rather for a market test. What works best? Let the consumer decide.

A more important question is standards. The few, very few, successful public high schools all have three things in common: vigorous discipline, strong leadership and high standards. Does it really work to abandon academic excellence as a standard for our children? Must all classes plod along at the level of the dullest child so that socializing goals will be met and no child will be left behind? Does it work to subject them to years of boredom in a computer-checked, limited, see-Spot-run vocabulary—or do we want to challenge them, test them, bring out their best with work and reading that is above their present abilities? The standard of excellence demands a challenge. The goal of socializing resists and defuses any real academic effort. Before you rush to take sides, there is something to be said for both positions. What we can say is that they cannot coexist. The one thing we cannot afford is a monolithic system that permits no choice between the two—which is what we have. Only the market permits the diversity we need, for high performance schools available to the academically inclined, and schools with more vocational goals in mind. In any case, the market should sort it out, not the essentially political, winner-takes-all decisions necessary in public schools.

The question I think most important of all is the teaching of values. Here, the monolithic nature of the public school system is at its worst, and is our worst enemy. For political reasons, curricula have been stripped of any hint of religious influence, even as history. The censorship goes much further than this. Traditional moral and ethical values have also been expelled from the classroom, and teaching is *supposed* to be "value-free." But this is madness. A primary purpose of education is precisely to transmit our values from generation to generation. Says Robert Maynard Hutchins, "If the object of education is the improvement of man, then any system of education that is without values is a contradiction in terms. A system that seeks bad values is bad. A system that denies the existence of values denies the possibility of education." Our present system combines the worst possibilities: in the guise of denying the existence of real values, it is smuggling in the teaching of bad values. Hutchins had no doubt that if unchecked, this would lead to the destruction of the West, nor do I. There is little or nothing we can do about it in the public schools, for they are politically controlled. Restoring the teaching of values would require a seachange in our national thought and the reversal of several landmark Supreme Court decisions. It will not be done; or if it is, it will take generations. Again, the only answer is private schooling, where values can be and still are taught. The market will oblige your demand for the values you want to pass along to your children. The market alone offers the diversity for competing desires to be satisfied. All religions may offer their own schools, as may any other interest or movement. In the one-size-fits-all bureaucratic system, no one is satisfied.

Ten years ago, I wrote:

> Government control of the American educational process is not the answer. A look at the outcome of the current educational system proves that values, standards and self-respect simply cannot exist with the present-day politicized system of learning. Past experience clearly shows that genuine education and government education are a contradiction in terms. So what's to be done to reestablish a system which will instill within our future leaders value and respect for the American ideal? The answer must come from the private sector. Why the private sector? Because the attributes, values and concerns of this group are synonymous with, rather than contradictory to, the aims of genuine education. Education must offer challenge and variety to awaken the *individual* conscience and draw forth unique qualities and capacities. Looking for the best in others and allowing their free development, letting people be themselves, afford each the opportunity to achieve his own potential. Such a view of education implies no "system," no "establishment," in the usual sense, but rather guidance by the private sector.

As you gather, I haven't changed my mind! I stand by every word and I think the case is even more urgent today. We cannot go on forever with our befuddled resort to socialized education. The first task of the educator is liberation. The individual needs to be freed from his limitations in order to develop his full potential and personhood. This is the most radical presumption of all. Only in freedom can unique individuals pursue their own, unique potentialities. Students differ in their capacities, interests and goals. True education must ever recognize distinctions and differences. It cannot be party to the barren ideological demand for equality. The diversity that we need to bring out the best in each young man and woman can only be had in the private sector. Our task in education is not to indoctrinate, especially not in whatever the presently fashionable dogmas prove to be. Our task instead is to teach our students how to learn and how to think for themselves. As Emerson wrote, "Cannot we let people be themselves, and enjoy life in their own way? You are trying to make that man another you. One's enough."

The role of the citizen and leader is exactly the same as that of the educator: liberate. All of us must strive to break the dead grip of a politicized and deathly ill school system. We can all contribute, even if it is no more than a rock-solid conviction that the present "system" of education is a disaster and cannot be anything else. Ideas have consequences! Add to this our conviction that character, maturity and responsibility are best developed in our young people when they are encouraged to pursue their *individual* talents in a framework of fixed truth and of a definite right and wrong—a framework that cannot be bent or trampled by current political whims or ideologies. No such education is possible in a bureaucratized state system, but private and genuine education will and must respond to our convictions. Our duty to do our parts, each and all, to restore freedom for education, is plain. Our conviction is strong. The purveyors of state "education" have everything fouled up, as usual. It is up to us to do things right.

Chapter VI

BLIGHT IN THE GROVES OF ACADEME

Elementary and secondary education are not alone in their problems. Consider higher education:

> Welcome to all of you who seek after the profound interpersonal dynamic which is Dartmouth. I trust all of you spent your summer break pursuing complex social dynamisms wherever they led. Let's give ourselves a round of applause for daring to be the courageous dreamers of the diverse oneness that is Dartmouth. How Special (capital S) we are.
>
> We must promote and strengthen our autointellectualism, mature our other-directed sensibilities and understand our public and private selves. I hope you will come away from your years at Dartmouth able to deeply appreciate and, indeed, feel the amness of of and the ofness of am in all its rich dimensions.
>
> Always remember: I am, you are, we be a community!
>
> —Snippet from a satire on a typical convocation address at Dartmouth, published by the *Dartmouth Review*.

The *Dartmouth Review* spoof didn't work. Art was imitating life much too closely. Seasoned observers, seeing this excerpt or the likes, could readily believe that the words had indeed been uttered by President Freedman of Dartmouth. Or it might have been by some other president of an Ivy League or prestige school, though admittedly Dartmouth is hard to beat in these matters. All too often we hear gibberish spoken in what should be the halls of higher education; and it is pretty hard to tell one piece of gibberish from another. No wonder satirizing it fails. Caution: you are about to enter the ofness and amness of American higher education in all its auto-intellectualism, other-directed sensibilities and diverse oneness.

Come along with me and let's look into a few cages, especially in the humanities departments.

From a letter to the editor concerning a major university, which shall be nameless to protect the guilty:

> I suggest you obtain a copy of the 1982 [yearbook]. It has pictures of the football team nude in the locker room. The [yearbook] staff is pictured in the nude. There is a picture of a nude student tied to an anchor while girls judge him on a scale.
>
> There are articles on the glories of cohabitation and the troubles of the gays.
>
> The dorms reek of marijuana. There is so much noise a student can't study. The boys and girls are in the same dorms without any supervision.

One wonders whether the students who are unable to study are missing much at such a school.

How about some results of high school and college education, from a National Geographic Society poll? This was no trivial sampling; 10,820 people in nine countries were polled. Four out of five of the Americans polled had at least a high school education. On the American home team, half said they had an atlas, nearly a third said they had a globe of the world, about half said they were fluent in a second language, and three-quarters professed a lively interest in geography. They finished seventh out of the nine, edging out Italy and Mexico. In the 18 to 24 age bracket, they finished dead last.

Among the American respondents, 95 percent knew that Washington, D.C., was the capital. Only 64 people missed that question. From there it goes straight downhill. Only half could locate New York state on a map. Only two-thirds could even read a map. Only three-quarters could tell north from south, or east from west. Finding Central America stumped 45 percent, 46 percent could not find Japan, 48 percent could not find France, and 75 percent could not find the Persian Gulf. Apart from this poll, it was noted in another report that a significant part of the population does not think New Mexico is in America. Does anybody teach geography anymore?

At least one outstanding high school student is heading for college with much too clear a view of what education is all about today. I conceal all particulars to spare her any embarrassment, and will say only that I am talking about a young lady who was valedictorian of her class with a perfect 4.0 average. In her valedictory address, she wanted to say, "The most important thing in life is not whether you have a good education or a good job, but whether you have the Lord in your life." School officials pressured her not to say that. When she refused to change her remarks, they prohibited her from speaking.

The same religious intolerance, doubled and redoubled, awaits the young lady throughout the "higher education" industry. And as a 4.0 student, she surely is smart enough to know it. I don't worry about her, but I do worry about very large numbers of young people marching unawares into a pitfall. They think they are going to get an education, and that it will give them an edge in life. It is the thing to do, after all. But they are defenseless against the wolves in academe who prey on innocent sheep. They have been given little by their public, bureaucratic schooling. They may have deep convictions of right and wrong instilled at home, yet could end up in short order rolling joints, buying condoms from vending machines and drinking the wisdom of Marxist teachers. Is this what you want for your daughter or son?

It is a central function of all education to transmit values. Schooling that fails to do so is unworthy of being called education. High schools and colleges that actively discourage "having the Lord in your life" are guilty of something much worse: the imposition of false and immoral values.

* * *

Here are remarks by Steven Wozniak, a founder of Apple Computer, about going back to school at the University of California, Berkeley:

I was going under an assumed name, Rocky Clark, so they didn't know who I was. I took a computer science course, economics, statistics and a few other courses. . . . My economics course was interesting. . . . We had a socialist T.A. [teaching assistant] who taught us that companies made money by cheating the consumer. All the kids in the class thought that companies would make a lot of profit if they could figure out a way to make it cheap and [rip off] the consumer. I contrast that with the way we did things at Apple. Every product design decision was based on what consumers wanted, what would compete the best, what they would buy. We tried to do what customers wanted in our best judgment and give them high-quality products. So I would stand up in class and argue about what the T.A. was saying. After a while he started telling me to shut up or that he would kick me out if I interrupted him again.

* * *

Mr. Dwight Lahr, dean at Dartmouth College, went on and on introducing his distinguished speaker. Her "life is an example of how one committed black woman activist has chosen to make a difference." Among her many accomplishments that Dean Lahr noted, she had won a Lenin Peace Prize. That's L-E-N-I-N, V.I., founder by armed force of the predominant terrorist state of this century, the U.S.S.R. I mention it so you won't confuse a Lenin Peace Prize with a Nobel Peace Prize, N-O-B-E-L, or V. I. Lenin with John Lennon. Lenin is estimated to have killed three million people establishing the first communist state. Small change, to be sure, compared to his successor, Stalin, who may have killed as many as thirty to fifty million. But then, killing three million people is not to be sneezed at. It is a record that would make any serial murderer in America gasp with envy. Lenin also invented large-scale concentration camps—an idea Nazi Germany made very progressive use of twenty years later. For these considerable achievements, Lenin's remains—stuffed like a prize muskie by a taxidermist—now lie on view in a veritable shrine in Moscow. His skin is too pale, says Ted Turner, but what does he know?

Dean Lahr drones on. Finally: "It gives me great pleasure to introduce Angela Davis, who will address us on the topic, 'Women, Race and Class.'"

Angela Davis is one of the best-known communists in America. In her interesting career, she made the FBI's ten-most-wanted list and was arrested and tried for complicity in murder, but got off with the help of some fancy legal talent. Then it was off to the Soviet Union for the Grand Tour, the Lenin Prize, and a bully pulpit from which to damn America and all its works. She ran for vice president, twice, on the Communist Party ticket, despite her distaste for the U.S. government in which she sought office. Dartmouth swooned over her. But first it took the sensible precaution of barring reporters. (That didn't work; her remarks were recorded anyway. Sample: "The Bush campaign is literally saturated with right-wingers, racists, fascists and Nazis.") She received a standing ovation.

The occasion was the fifteenth anniversary of Dartmouth turning coeducational, in 1973, when that was the trendy thing to do in the prestige schools. Hillsdale did it nearly a century and a half earlier, at its founding in 1844, when it was still a new, radical and daring advance. Only one other college, Oberlin, admitted women before Hillsdale. But Dartmouth was not embarrassed to celebrate its belated conversion, nor embarrassed to select Angela Davis to lead the festivities: with a call to abolish the kind of society that makes Dartmouth possible.

Selecting a conservative speaker in such schools gets quite a different reaction. Such distinguished guests as former Defense Secretary Casper Weinberger, Contra leader Adolfo Calero and former U.N. Ambassador Jeane Kirkpatrick have had to cancel speaking invitations and have even been physically prevented from speaking at Berkeley, Columbia, Smith and Harvard. They have been heckled, threatened with violence, showered with debris and shouted down. The student "activists" responsible are seldom if ever disciplined.

So much for open-mindedness, academic freedom and scholarly inquiry. So much for "daring to be the courageous dreamers of the diverse oneness. . . . " On some campuses, the "diversity" ranges all the way from Maoist to Stalinist. But at least you can be sure your child will be given a Safe Sex kit upon arriving, and that there will be a condom vending machine in the dorm.

Meanwhile, there is the question of academics, if any, on today's campus. What sort of education can your son or daughter get? Mixed with how much leftist indoctrination? With tuitions ranging from $3,000 to $20,000 per year, it's worth looking into.

One of the hot items in modern scholarship is called Popular Culture, and includes such courses as "Introduction to Rock 'n' Roll." A professor who teaches it argues that you can learn more by listening to the Grateful Dead than you can by "looking at the stained glass-windows of the cathedral at Chartres." It is just as well that Henry Adams, author of *Mont-Saint-Michel and Chartres,* is no longer among us, or the professor could call his next course "Eating Crow."

Just for the flavor of it, here are some papers delivered at a gathering of Popular Culture teachers. They have a nice scholarly ring to them, don't you think? "Body Slam: Professional Wrestling as Greek Drama." (Sample: "The first step toward a just appreciation of wrestling involves a return to an aesthetics that discards modern notions of authenticity or truth and embraces notions of mimesis that are more in line with those of a Johnson or an Aristotle.") "Marketing Odor: A Historical Analysis of Perfume Ads in Selected Magazines." "The Reconciliation of Archie and Meathead: *All in the Family*'s Last Episode." "The American Garage Sale and its Cultural Implications." "Yogi Berra: The Dumb Philosopher?" Finally, a paper that will surely play well in this part of the country: "The Final Four as Final Judgment: The NCAA Basketball Tournament." Panel discussions at the meeting covered such matters of concern as cooking literature, women in comic strips, and raunchy radio talk shows. There were five workshops devoted to cemetery architecture.

Of course, the modern institute of higher education teaches a great deal more than rock 'n' roll. Parents of college-bound youngsters would do well to peruse the college catalogue with care, tedious though it is. For instance, if you find no end of sociology courses and all of them sound as if they were being outlined by Mr. Freedman at Dartmouth, you're in trouble. ("How did you spend your summer vacation?" "I pursued complex social dynamisms wherever they led.") I can't give you much help here—it would take a separate and large book—but the more you see the words "social," "society" or variations, the more trouble you're in. The more references to races, class and gender (Angela Davis' theme and what Irving Kristol calls the "unholy trinity" saturating academic thinking), the more certain you can be that your child is in for both a debunking of your family values and a large dose of leftist indoctrination. Also beware of critical this, reevaluation of that, revisionist anything, or the like. Chances are high it will be an attack on the West.

By now you are probably wondering what happened to Socrates, Virgil, Augustine, Aquinas and Shakespeare, to Locke and Burke and Dr. Johnson and Adam Smith, to America's Founding Fathers and system of self-government. You are right to wonder. That's our next story.

* * *

Perhaps the most telling case of this kind, as I write, is that of Stanford University. Here, certainly, is one of the most prestigious and costly universities, whose achievements over the years have been top drawer. In recent years it has turned into a leftist fort, and if anyone wants to dispute that point, we will have a jolly time of it. You will have a hard time finding a Republican on the faculty and the Democrats you find are not the down-home kind in Vermont or Indiana or Arkansas.

The bare facts are that in 1980 (about a century late, but never mind) Stanford adopted a one-year course in Western Culture, which freshmen were required to take. The course was built on a core reading list of fifteen significant works of Western philosophy and literature, from ancient times to the present. It was said to be "immensely popular" with students. In the spring of 1986, a small but highly vocal group of students demanded that the course be abolished. Western civilization, they said (they must have been paying close attention in class), was laden with imperialism, racism, sexism, elitism, and maybe a few other "isms" I missed. Who were Aristotle and Rembrandt and Donne anyway but white males? (In the race-class-gender routine that passes for thinking nowadays, this is a crushing argument: anything written or created by white males is to be dismissed automatically as hopelessly biased. Marx, Lenin and Stalin are exempt, however.)

Imagine, all this enlightenment before Angela Davis passed along the same message to Dartmouth! The "diverse oneness" of it all sounds suspiciously like the old Party line.

Faced with a challenge to its liberal pedigree, Stanford has-
tened to cave in. It appointed a "task force" to "evaluate" the course.
All too predictably, the task force came up with a recommendation
to kill Western Culture and replace it with a new and also required
course called CIV: Culture, Ideas and Values. CIV tossed out much
of the Western heritage and replaced it with reading one book a
quarter written by "women, minorities and persons of color." I find
it obnoxious to hype academic work by virtue of the author's race,
class or gender (and liberalism agreed with me not many years ago),
but nowadays that is the in thing and the only thing. Jesse Jackson
speeded the adoption of CIV by leading students in a chant, "Hey,
hey, ho, ho, Western Culture's gotta go." His followers stressed the
point by taking over the Stanford president's office for five hours.
They also held strident demonstrations, disrupted classes and threatened the university. The final vote was 39–4 to terminate the Western Culture course. William Bennett, then Secretary of Education,
said of the ruckus: "The loudest voices won, not through force of
argument but through bullying, threatening and name-calling . . . a
great university was brought low by the very forces which modern
universities came into being to oppose—ignorance, irrationality and
intimidation."

Let us be clear here. The primary mission of education is to
transmit the knowledge, experience and values of our culture from
one generation to the next. This most certainly includes the testimony of "women, minorities and persons of color." But as certainly
it does *not* include killing off the essence of our way of life that
goes back thirty centuries; nor does it mandate a hostile attitude
toward the innumerable achievements, humane advances and moral
values of the West. The West has given the world science (which
never took root anywhere else, and could not have, without the
foundations of Western religious belief) and enormous progress in
human rights, literature, art, commerce, standard of living and
much more. It is the business of real education to transmit these
matters, not to trample them.

What actually was done away with, in favor of what else, at
Stanford? Here, for the flavor, are excerpts from a report in the
Wall Street Journal:

Stanford educators promised to replace [Western Culture] with something better, but now we're learning what they had in mind. . . . Of the 15 great works previously required, only six remain. The rest have been replaced by lesser known authors. Dante's *Inferno* is out, for example, but *I . . . Rigoberta Menchu* is in. This epic tracks Ms.Menchu's progress from poverty to Guatemalan revolutionary and "the effects of her feminist and socialist ideologies."

Aquinas and Thomas More are out, but *Their Eyes Were Watching God* by feminist Zora Neale Hurston is in. Ms. Hurston's book offers a critique of the male domination of American society. Locke and Mill go down the memory hole, replaced by such as the UN Declaration of Human Rights and Rastafarian poetry.

Virgil, Cicero and Tacitus give way to Frantz Fanon. Mr. Fanon's *The Wretched of the Earth* celebrates violent revolution and is praised on its own book jacket "as a veritable handbook of revolutionary practice and social reorganization." Plato's *Republic* is said to illustrate "anti-assimilationist movements," whatever they are. Martin Luther and Galileo are out, but such timeless notables as Juan Rulfo (*The Burning Plain*) and Sandra Cisneros (*The House on Mango Street*) are in. And so on.

For more flavor, here are some brief excerpts from the CIV prospectus issued by Stanford itself:

One of the main goals of this course [is to examine] culture in the context of complex relations between master and slave, colonizer and colonized, marginal and dominant, women and men. [See what I mean about gibberish?]

First quarter: The Spanish debate over indigenous rights raises issues around race as well as religion; readings on European enlightenment include Wollstonecraft on question of gender, and Flora Tristan on question of class. Race, gender and class are all thematized in Chungara de Barrios' autobiography and Anzaldua's poetic essays.

Second quarter: Race is a central focus of . . . Gender is a central issue in . . . Roumain's *Masters of the Dew* plays out a class drama . . .

Third quarter: Marx and Weber are essential sources on class; Frantz Fanon on race; gender, ethnicity and class are central themes in Rulfo, Menchu, Chavez and Anzaldua. [This could go on and on and on.]

You got the picture a long time ago, and a ten-year-old could hardly miss it at this point. "Hey, hey, ho, ho, Western Civ has got to go." Where it's going, at once-great Stanford, is straight over a cliff. Three thousand years of our Greek, Roman, Judaic and Christian heritage are simply thrown out, at a faculty meeting, in favor of a pure leftist agenda. Race, class, gender!

Naturally, that was not the end of the story. An assistant dean at Stanford wrote the *Journal* to protest that the new CIV course was just the thing! But the response from other readers was scathing, and nowhere more so than from Professor Allan Bloom, author of *The Closing of the American Mind*. "Mr. Fanon," he wrote, " . . . is a *demonstrably* inferior and derivative thinker to whom no one would pay any attention if he were not the ideologue of currently popular movements, and did not, as a black Algerian, fit Stanford's job description. Stanford students are to be indoctrinated with ephemeral ideologies and taught that there can be no intellectual resistance to one's own time and its passions. . . . I could hope for no more stunning confirmation of my thesis."

Mr. Navaratna S. Rajaram, who is a professor of industrial engineering in Texas, offered an unusual and wry perspective on the Stanford affair:

> Those Stanford University activists who want to change the orientation of the core course, Western Culture, might be interested to hear from someone like me who was born into a "non-Western" culture. Nearly all the knowledge of the past glories of these non-Western cultures—in which their intelligentsia take such great pride—is the result of Western scholarship. These cultures, for all their greatness, have little history and no archaeology. So they owe a great debt to Western culture.
>
> As a technocrat, perhaps I am guilty of too narrow an approach and the activists are actually right. If so, they might next time try to similarly broaden the scope of technological education. We could be designing boomerangs in aerospace engineering, studying gypsy fortune telling and Babylonian astrology in physics, using pebbles and the abacus in computer science and practicing West African voodoo in medical schools.

Exactly so. Are we prepared to go back to systems where a person is literally the property of a monarch, where women are chattels, where we never get enough to eat, where our status in life is determined by the sex, group, class or race one is born into? Only in the West have these horrible, historical abuses been conquered. Those who want to go back, or who are too ill-educated and ignorant to know what they propose, chant "Hey, hey, ho ho." But they have nothing to do with education. They are against it. They are destroying it.

James Jackson Kilpatrick, echoing Bennett, put the case very well. "We must study and nurture the West because it is our culture, because it is fundamentally good, because it is a source of incomparable intellectual complexity and diversity and depth, and because the West is under attack. Other cultures should be studied also—of course they should be studied!—but a thorough grounding in our own civilization has to come first." To which I say: amen.

That is the way things go on campuses great and small today. The 1960s radical student is now a tenured professor. It is said with some justice that the only believing Marxists remaining in all the world are in American universities. Bitter experience has decimated Marxist views in every country where they have been put into practice. But on many an American campus, they rule. The hard left has found a haven in the Groves of Academe, and is using it to work its worst on everything America—and the West—stand for. It is protected by academic tenure, by government "civil rights" rules that shelter everything from sexual deviancy to the radical agenda, by "affirmative action" to bring in its favored groups at the expense of academically better qualified candidates, and on and on. It is heavily funded by—*you*. Like it or not. Taxpayers are obliged to finance not only university operations and student grants, but also such campus activity as feminist groups, lesbian and gay groups, revolutionary groups, abortion counseling, and other things you may not approve of. That's another thing to keep in mind when your dear old alma mater asks you (or your company) for donations.

Consider the case of Georgetown University, in Washington, D.C., which is affiliated with the Roman Catholic Church. Back in 1977, the D.C. City Council, which has been called the most liberal legislative body this side of Sweden, passed an ordinance banning discrimination on every ground you can think of and some you wouldn't dream of. One of them was "sexual orientation."

Georgetown was immediately stuck between a rock and a hard

place. The church teaches that homosexuality is a mortal sin, condemned by the commandments of God. The message didn't get through to some Georgetown students. A Gay Rights Coalition was soon organized, and it demanded the same recognition, facilities and support that other student groups got. Georgetown refused. It could not have done otherwise without violating its own religious convictions and teaching. The students sued—and won. What the court actually said is that Georgetown did not have to recognize the Gay Rights Coalition "officially," but it did have to provide facilities and financial support. A great deal of litigation has passed since, and it is still going on as I write. Generally, the war is between Congress and the D.C. City Council. But it really is a detail in the larger picture we have discussed: what happens to a college or university when it gets trapped by government money? The answer is, it becomes a vassal of government. That is why we have protected our independence at Hillsdale so fiercely, and at such cost.

At Hillsdale, we offer a solid liberal arts education in traditional form to any qualified applicant. We think it is a fine education for developing each individual. The state is not going to dictate our curriculum, ever. Nobody but nobody is going to tell us what we can or cannot teach.

Poor Georgetown was snared by tax dollars, and now it must indulge, foster and support a group whose practices are sinful and obnoxious to its own religious beliefs. I'm sorry and it is unjust, but at this stage in our far-too-officious public life, the only way out is to remain determinedly private. The cost in dollars and vexation is very high, but unless the government rethinks and repeals its control, there is no other choice for the educator.

Whatever were the oracles thinking of when they decreed two decades ago that the federal bureaucracy could dispense higher education in America?

We must conclude this unhappy tour of higher education. I could give you many more examples of its many ills, and there will be more examples next year and the year after. But we have seen enough. Back in 1978 I wrote:

The results of progressive education have been ugly, on campus and off campus, but a word of warning is in order. However reprehensible our present college and university may have become, . . . we must beware of the tendency to use political power in correcting the situation. The autonomous university community has usually been a seat of traditional values and a haven for the individual against church and king. At its best it can again be such a haven against the assaults of democratic politicization. In fact, our present discontents are largely due to the extent to which we have accepted political authority (financing, standards, controls, values) in an institutional area where that authority does not belong.

Not only do I stand by every word of that, I must add: the situation is much worse. The level of political intrusion remains a near-perfect measure of all that ails higher education today. There is not a single case we have looked at that is not largely traceable to political and ideological intervention into traditional education. That level of intrusion is much higher than even ten years ago. Federal funding has increased sharply (despite what you've heard in the media). As in any largely bureaucratic monopoly, heavy funding multiplies inefficiencies and costs soar. For at least a decade and probably longer, the price of going to college has been rising twice as fast as the cost of living. This invites the politicians to "help" with more of your money, and they have been very "helpful" indeed. Three dollars out of every four in student aid come from the federal government. The government virtually owns higher education. The primary role of a university president is begging: "incessant, nonstop shrill demands for more and more money," as Robert Nisbet put it.

Secretary Bennett, addressing these matters at *Harvard* of all places (a courageous man!), said: "I have never seen a greater interest in money. These higher education lobbyists put Harvard Square hawkers to shame." He went on: "They are . . . very good at getting their funds from a Congress seemingly cowed by the pieties and pontifications and poor-mouthings of American higher education, but very few words can be heard from any of these representatives about . . . purpose, quality, curriculum, the moral authority and responsibilities of universities."

The converse is, the independence of the higher education

community sinks ever lower. The quality of education sinks with it. Even worse, the moral authority of education has been eroded from within, frittered away and attacked until it is at the vanishing point. We have destroyed standards and eliminated the teaching of moral values in the public school years. We send our children defenseless into colleges and universities where they are more likely to be indoctrinated in obnoxious doctrines than to be uplifted and helped in their development by the "grand old fortifying curriculum."

In a word, higher education is a mess, or worse, a menace, and I see only one way out. We must understand what education is. We must understand that a good deal of the activity in colleges and universities is not education as it has been known and understood over hundreds of years. We may call it education but it is not. Any education worthy of the name must focus on the individual. It must transmit to students, one at a time, the wisdom and truth and moral value of our heritage. It must help individuals develop their uniqueness and critical capacities. It must show them "the best that has been thought and said." This is what we strive to do at Hillsdale. But, sadly, education in this, its traditional form, is heading for extinction in America. It is being done in by thinking that sees only groups and never individuals; that sees only race, class and gender—"the unholy trinity." It is being done in by political intrusion that is equally imposed in terms of groups and categories and rules. In this atmosphere and from the premises of group thinking, genuine education is not possible.

I repeat, the only way we can be sure our children get a real education is to start with an understanding of what it is. I have given you the bad news here, too much of it. We have seen what isn't education. The good news is that, together, we can restore and improve education: at least for our own children and for all who want something better than the "higher education" industry provides. We'll see how next. Private effort has quietly worked a few miracles toward the goal we share, and we can do more.

Chapter VII

THERE IS AN ANSWER
TO OUR EDUCATIONAL WOES

The following is an imaginary interview with Adam Smith, the first and greatest economist. His remarks on the economics of education are of particular interest to us, for Smith was himself a teacher; indeed, one of world renown. He was a professor of moral philosophy, a man of the highest standing. Despite his speech problem, he attracted students from thousands of miles away and in a time when such travel was slow, costly and dangerous. His ideas were of such power that they swept through Europe with tidal force for a century. Many a decaying monarchy fell before them, and many a nation was freed of its feudal past. For this, Smith was called the principal legislator of Europe. Published in the same year as our Declaration of Independence, his ideas soon traveled across the Atlantic and helped give life and health to the new American republic. Jefferson, among others, received them warmly.

It is my questions that are imaginary. Smith's "answers" are from his epochal *Wealth of Nations* (1776). His style was a model of precision in its time, but may seem verbose now. Bear with it. I have shortened his sentences where possible; the words and thoughts remain his.

GR: Professor Smith, what is the correct way to finance education?

AS: The institutions for the education of the youth may furnish a revenue sufficient for defraying their own expense. The fee or honorary which the scholar pays to the master naturally constitutes a revenue of this kind.

GR: In America, we no longer have any concept that education is a service to be provided by the teacher, in the market, for fees or tuition.

AS: In [some] universities the teacher is prohibited from receiving any honorary or fee from his pupils, and his salary constitutes the whole revenue which he derives from his office. His interest is, in this case, set as directly in opposition to his duty as it is possible to set it.

GR: Paycheck *vs.* duty! Tell us more. That is how our whole system is run.

AS: It is the interest of every man to live as much at his ease as he can; and if his emoluments are to be precisely the same, whether he does, or does not perform some very laborious duty, it is certainly his interest either to neglect it altogether, or to perform it in as careless and slovenly a manner as [school] authority will permit.

GR: You say matters get even worse when the faculty is given undue authority over working conditions and spending. Would you explain?

AS: They are likely to make a common cause, to be all very indulgent to one another, and every man to consent that his neighbor might neglect his duty, [if] he is allowed to neglect his own. In the University of Oxford, the greater part of the public professors have, for these many years, given up even the pretence of teaching.

GR: It is usually the state paying their salaries. Why doesn't the state step in and make them work?

AS: An extraneous jurisdiction of this kind is liable to be exercised both ignorantly and capriciously. . . . [Also] the person subject to such jurisdiction is necessarily degraded by it, and, instead of being one of the most respectable, is rendered one of the meanest and most contemptible persons in the society.

GR: That describes many an American university! Things are not much better in the high schools. Do you think students should be forced to attend by truancy laws?

AS: Where the masters really perform their duty, there are no examples, I believe, that the students ever neglect theirs. No discipline is ever requisite to force attendance upon lectures which are really worth the attending.

GR: The state uses certification to protect public schools from competition by private schools. Have you any comment?

AS: Schools have no exclusive privileges. In order to obtain the honors of graduation, it is not necessary that a person should bring a certificate of his having studied a certain number of years at a public school. If upon examination he appears to understand what is taught there, no questions are asked about the place he learned it.

GR: In high school, curricula are largely dictated by the state, and tend to serve the purposes of the state. They deny individuality and moral values in favor of conformity and socialization.

AS: Were there no public institutions for education, no system, no science would be taught for which there was not some demand. A private teacher could never find his account [i.e., employment] in teaching an exploded or antiquated system, or a science universally believed to be a mere useless and pedantic heap of sophistry and nonsense.

GR: What else should we know about state financing of education?

AS: The diligence of public teachers is corrupted by circumstances which render them independent of success and reputation. Their salaries put the private teacher who would [compete] with them [in the same fix as private enterprises trying to compete with state-subsidized enterprises]. The endowments of schools and colleges have, in this manner, not only corrupted the diligence of public teachers, but have rendered it almost impossible to have any good private ones.

GR: Hillsdale College has to face just such unfair competition, and it is a major problem. Today, high school students are under great pressure to spend four or more years in college—most often at the huge state universities, because they are cheaper.

AS: Whatever forces a certain number of students to any college or university, independent of the merit or reputation of the teachers, tends to diminish the necessity of that merit or reputation. . . . Those parts of education, it is to be observed, for the teaching of which there are no public institutions, are generally the best taught.

GR: That goes back to education as a market service. But all of our professors are salaried now, and a startling amount of the funding on most campuses is from taxes. . . .

AS: Even where the reward of the master does not arise altogether from [fees], it still is not necessary that it should be derived from [the] general revenue of the society. . . . Through the greater part of Europe, accordingly, the endowment of schools and colleges makes either no charge upon that general revenue, or but a very small one.

GR: No federal taxes needed for either public schools or higher education? Oh, my! This is going to blow a whole century's worth of progressive education scams.

AS: The most essential parts of education, to read, write and account, can be acquired at so early a period of life that those even [in] the lowest occupations have time to acquire them. The public can facilitate this acquisition by establishing in every parish or district a little school, where children may be taught for a reward so moderate that even a common laborer may afford it; the master being partly, but not wholly paid by the public; because, if he was wholly, or even principally paid by it, he would soon learn to neglect his business.

GR: I myself was lucky enough to attend a one-room school, and see what you mean. But all the so-called reform ideas of our time demand bigger and bigger schools, fancier equipment and more money—all for our own good, of course.

AS: I have never known much good done by those who affected to trade for the public good.

GR: Thank you, Professor Smith. You give us pause. We have much to think about as we face our own problems in education.

The Market Principle in Education

Our object in this discussion is to find what does work in education. Elsewhere, we toured the minefields of American education, from elementary schools through the universities. Our public schools are a costly, bureaucratic mistake. Many of our colleges and universities are more eager to pursue tax dollars and left-wing ideology than to dispense anything worthy of being called higher education. It is a depressing tour. We have here listened to the expert diagnosis of Adam Smith on the roots of educational failure, because the road to success begins with understanding what is going wrong with our present arrangements.

Smith was a man able to reel off centuries of history in defense of his thinking; a man who by sheer force of intellect conceived what had never been known: free markets. Not only did he conceive them, he made them possible by arguing that "natural liberty" is the most just and productive status of mankind. In liberty, he said, private interest is led by an invisible hand to serve the public good, and everyone benefits. Just as surely, the general welfare is harmed by protectionist and special interest schemes imposed with the connivance of the state. We know from long and sometimes bitter experience how right Smith was in these points. We see here that his principles apply as much to education as to international trade.

To review quickly, education is, or should be, a market business. The school market in principle begins with a single educator offering his services for a fee, to any who wish to learn what he can teach. More familiarly, it takes the form of a school in which several teachers offer instruction in a rounded curriculum, for which they are paid tuition. In either case, the market basis for his work imposes a discipline on the educator that is absent if he is fully salaried and not accountable to his customer, the student. Students select their teachers in the fields they wish to study and pay accordingly. As in any market, the best, most productive, hardest-working teachers will attract the most lucrative clientele and command the best fees. But in the absence of market discipline, teachers collude to reduce each other's workload to a minimum (and in our own times, to coerce higher salaries for this shoddy work with strikes). Teachers who get their paycheck whether or not they perform well will perform as poorly as permitted. If they are still ambitious, they cannot improve their lot by extra effort in the classroom, so they will apply their energy to other enterprises. Outside authority over these practices is likely to be arbitrary and harmful; bureaucrats do not know what education is or how to produce it. In the bureaucratic scheme, teachers are reduced to serfs, albeit well-fattened ones, with only two options: they must get political protection, or they must survive by "obsequiousness," fawning over the powers above them. (We have seen massive traffic up both avenues.) Nothing about our present arrangements would have surprised Adam Smith!

In plain words, it is the consumer who should dictate the content and quality of education, as in any business. The reason that public schoolteachers can strike and that college professors can peddle utopian nonsense is the same: They don't have to earn their pay by satisfying the consumer. Where the would-be buyer of education is not given a choice; where taxes and truancy laws and other statist measures like certification force young people into the public school system; where teachers can bank a paycheck without any reference to their own market value, the stage is set for a disaster. And disaster is just what we are buying, at a cost of hundreds of billions a year, by trying to defy market principles.

The only real and enduring solution to our educational woes is to restore the market. The answer is that simple. There is no other. Every problem we face in education is traceable to the same circumstance: the schools are run by a socialist bureaucracy instead of consumers. Of course, changing is not simple at all. I can hear the screams from coast to coast at the very idea of privatizing education. We will be told that education is so very, very important we can't even think of leaving it to private enterprise. This argument would make sense if government schools were the only way to get a good education, and private schools could not do the job. The truth is exactly the other way around. Adam Smith heard all this in his time too. In fact he reserved some of his choicest scorn for the squeals of monopolists getting yanked off the trough. "If a [member of Congress] opposes them [monopolists], and still more if he has the authority to be able to thwart them, neither the most acknowledged probity, nor the highest rank, nor the greatest public service, can protect him from the most infamous abuse and detraction . . . arising from the insolent outrage of furious and disappointed monopolists." Stand by for some infamous abuse and outrage. George Roche (pronounced like the insect) has done it again.

But I do not propose anything unusual, and I know I do not stand alone. What is more important, we at Hillsdale have been competing with the monopolists for many years, yet we survive and flourish. The right way to do things really does work. We had to face down the biggest bureau in the world to prove it, but we're still free and doing fine. And we are intently aware why we do well: because Hillsdale has done everything in its power to remain private, and hence to offer a real education on classical terms in the marketplace. We sell our services. We don't force them on anyone. And we don't take tax subsidies. We manage because we sell good education. The entirely *voluntary*, private support provided by tuition and contributions constitutes a market transaction. All faculty salaries, scholarships, buildings, (as well as everything else at Hillsdale) come from private, voluntary market sources. We know we are at an extreme disadvantage against the thousands of heavily tax-subsidized colleges and universities, and we have every right to resent it. But we know their "system" won't produce real education. I'm not crying about it. For those of you with eyes to see and ears to hear, this is opportunity.

Windows for Schooling

This fall, as American parents watched Marxist socialism take off its clothes and collapse in Eastern Europe, they cheerfully sent 41 million children back into the care of one of the most socialist enterprises in the Western world, that $180 billion near-monopoly known as U.S. public education.
—Warren T. Brookes

The amount we are forced to spend on public education in this country exceeds the Gross National Product in most countries of the world. What we get for all of our trouble is a system that puts our children dead last, or close to it, in scholastic competition with almost any others, almost anywhere. They have lost in competitions with places you never heard of (assuming you too had a public school education). When they go head to head with, say, Japan, where education is taken seriously, the results are almost too painful to report. For instance, the *average* Japanese math student does better than our math whizzes—the top five percent. We have discussed many such matters earlier, and I have thick folders of more of the same—but it is all too melancholy. Let's look at how we too do it right, or did, once upon a time.

Some years ago, a lady named Avis Carlson wrote a memoir titled *Small World Long Gone: A Family Record of an Era*. Among her recollections was this: "At that point in the history of Kansas education [1907], the county superintendents had a rite known as County Eighth Grade Examinations, which was, I think, the sole standardized achievement test in the whole state system." She describes the test at some length. Here are a few examples:

"The 'orthography' quiz asked us to spell 20 words, including 'abbreviated,' 'obscene,' 'elucidation,' 'assassination,' and 'animosity.' We were also required to 'make a table' showing the different sounds of all the vowels. . . . Among the other eight questions (each subject had 10 questions) was one which asked us to 'divide into syllables and mark diacritically the words 'profuse, retrieve, rigidity, defiance, priority, remittance and propagate.'

"Two of Arithmetic's ten questions asked us to find the interest on an eight percent note for $900 running two years, two months, six days; and also to reduce three pecks, five quarts, one pint to bushels.

"In History we were to 'give a brief account of the colleges, printing and religion in the Colonies prior to the American Revolution,' to 'name the principal campaigns and military leaders of the Civil War,' and to 'name the principal political questions which have been advocated since the Civil War and the party which advocated each.'"

She had similar examples in reading, pronunciation, word meanings, geography, physiology, grammar and so on. This was a test that would stump many a college graduate today, and in fact, many teachers. Avis Carlson passed it at age 11 years, 8 months in a one-room schoolhouse in Kansas in 1907. As we confront the disastrous condition of public schooling today, here is, at least, the comfort of knowing we once did it far better, in small inexpensive facilities, by teachers who know what as well as how to teach. But was this example a fluke? By no means.

An acquaintance sent me a copy of his grandfather's teaching certificate, dated 1895. It sets forth the teaching requirements for secondary education, first to eighth grade, in a small rural school in Wisconsin. Teachers were tested in: Orthoepy, orthography (the studies of pronunciation and spelling), reading, penmanship, arithmetic, English grammar, geography, U.S. history, the state constitution, the federal Constitution, physiology and hygiene, theory and art of teaching, grammatical analysis, physiology, physical geography and elementary algebra. For high school teaching, higher algebra, geometry and natural philosophy were also required. It was noted on the certificate that the gentleman had attended "Teachers' Institute" for five days. Note that this is only the "core" curriculum, as we would put it now, for all teachers. There were many other subjects offered at the high school level.*

This rigorous curriculum would be front-page news if it were offered in any public school in the country today; yet it was the norm a century ago all across America, even in dusty little farm-town schools attended by barefoot children. Remarkably, teachers were all required to know the entire curriculum. After all, they might be called on to teach all eight grades in a little one-room schoolhouse (as I was taught). They got very little training in *how* to teach: five days in the Teachers' Institute sufficed in this case. Rather, they concentrated on basic subject matter, and did so by attending to their own education. They could and often did take

---

*Here is the curriculum at a four-year high school in the midwest in 1910: Algebra, Ancient History, Botany, Literary Readings, Physical Geography, Composition, Bookkeeping, Mediaeval History, Physiology, Zoology, English History, Geometry, American Literature, German, Greek, American History, Civics, Economics, Physics, English Literature, Theory and Art of Teaching, Psychology, Manual Training, Mechanical Drawing.

their teaching posts straight out of high school, after being rigor-
ously tested.

I wonder just how much we have lost by turning this whole
procedure upside-down. Nowadays, would-be teachers usually must
spend years in education schools at the universities, which are primarily devoted to theories of education, not subject matter. They
often go back for higher degrees in more of the same, which earns
them quicker promotions in the bureaucratic pay scales. (The textbooks they use are full of the same mush.) And they end up special-
izing in one or two subjects, which some never master as well as a
teacher a century ago who could handle the whole curriculum.

The results of this we all know too well. Students graduate
without learning a core curriculum and go on to become the next
generation of teachers with little to impart to their own students.
The level of education keeps going down and down. But more is
lost than this. We have traded in the high morale and moral values
of good, basic and *successful* schooling for a bureaucratized anthill
whose focus is on money, gimmicks, theory, power and more
money. No amount of tinkering with a system like that is ever going
to help. No amount of extra dollars will help it either, and there are
scores of studies to back up the point.

It may be objected that I am contradicting myself: the little red
schoolhouses were public, not private, yet they did very well. True,
but they were market schools in almost every sense. Attendance
was not required, so schools had to perform. Moreover, they were
accountable to their customers, the community of parents, in a
direct, no-nonsense way. They were held to high moral standards
by the community, both in enforcing discipline and in what they
taught. There is no comparing schools like this with the ones we
have today, which are operated by bureaucratic rules, have no moral
standards at all, and are barely accountable to anyone.

Couldn't we go back to the old ways? I'm afraid not; not, at
least, without undoing generations of bad law, bureaucracy and
education theory. I can't see any chance of this. For example,
Christian morality was freely taught in school of old, built into
subject lessons. In this, the little red schoolhouse fulfilled its basic
educational duty to transmit our values to the younger generation.

Today, this is strictly illegal. The least whiff of anything to do with religion is barred from the schoolgrounds. I don't believe this law will be reversed until the last liberal has died off and all liberal dogmas have been forgotten. For a second example, the schools' success depends on their being freed of bureaucracy. This is too much to hope for. Nothing on earth is harder to get rid of than bureaucracy, and nowhere on earth is there more of it than in the public school system. There are plenty of other problems as well, and I see no way around them today unless we turn back to private schools.

What will help, and where the market lies, is precisely in the basic schooling that was once a birthright. The door is wide open for private entrepreneurs who can deliver what the average country teacher could in 1895 or 1907.

This is a tough order, make no mistake. The content of a good core curriculum has not been lost to us, nor have the means and techniques of effective teaching. But much has been lost in our times, both in and out of the classroom, that is of utmost importance to sound schooling. The self-indulgence of the "Me" generation won't do at all. The whole mindset of public schools and "educationists" has to go. The classroom is not a laboratory for social or political experiments, nor the right place to solve social problems.

The keys to sound schooling start at home, in strong family ties based on old-fashioned values. Even now, children from the family that stays together manage to salvage some education, no matter how bad their school. You and I, as parents, must give our children the values of self-discipline, responsibility and plain old hard work. If they slack off or misbehave, it is up to us to straighten them out immediately. Values rarely mentioned, but equally important in school, are good manners, a sense of humility, obedience and respect for one's elders. Children from Vietnamese or other Asian families in which all these values are cultivated at home do dumbfoundingly well in school, despite their handicap in having to learn English.

Families that share these concerns always soon become what Edmund Burke called one of the "little platoons" of community, or we might say nowadays, a support group, that will help and guide their children's school. I am not talking about PTA meetings or athletic boosters or committees trying to change bad textbooks or curricula in public schools (fat chance when bureaucrats dictate both). I mean the moral force of the parental community. This is a real community, joining teachers and administrators to reach shared moral goals. Or if that sounds too fancy, suppose a kid starts taking drugs—*wham*! the whole group comes down on his head until he wises up. It is that simple and it works. I cannot cite a single scientific study to prove it, but I know it works and it is a big part of making your school a success. A good school will be the center of a moral community.

Finally, let's bring back the old-fashioned headmaster and the dedicated teacher. Public school principals, not to mention superintendents, are awash in bureaucracy. Their real business should be teaching, and making sure that the teachers in their charge teach well—not administrative paperwork. We need very little administration: only that of the independent school itself or of whatever business or church runs it. We do not need *any* local, state, federal or United Nations educational bureaucracy. We will save billions by eliminating "Departments of Education" at every governmental level. All we need is schoolmarms and masters, and a headmaster or headmistress to keep an eye on things.

And where will we find these extinct species? Oh, my—an easy question at last. We have them now. There are thousands of wonderful teachers trapped in the public education monopoly and hating it. Offer them a market wage (a salary cut) and freedom to teach as they see fit, and you will have all the applicants you can handle. The teachers' autonomy in their own classrooms is paramount, and future headmasters-to-be will know it. Both go from bureaucratic suffocation to a real market for their skills and services, and if they can deliver the goods, they love it. It is the weak and incompetent who hide behind the skirts of teachers' unions. Many with greater dedication and skill long to be free. I know from firsthand experience. We have been able to hire a truly outstanding faculty at Hillsdale College simply because they come here to teach in their own way, and can escape the bleak bureaucracy at State U.

I could not be more proud of these multi-talented men and women who have joined us.

Start your private school with a promise of freedom and fair treatment to good teachers. If that bleeds all the talent out of the socialist school system, it won't bother me one bit. School, I repeat, should be a free and competitive market like any other. The consumer should be able to shop and choose, and not have a hopelessly inferior school forced upon him through the tax mechanism. But here's a little secret. Get in quick, while there is still a rich sellers' market created by the awful socialist education we endure—socialism is dying all over the world, and may even die here some day. You'd better be there first and steal all the good teachers by offering them real freedom to teach.

Of course we are not all cut out to start up, or teach in, private schools, but we can all help and encourage those who do. I leave you with this thought, plainly put as always by Milton Friedman: "If your corporation goes out to buy a valve, you don't ask, 'Is there somebody who went to the same school I did that produces that valve?' You ask, 'Who is producing the valve that will serve the interests of my company best, that will fit into my product best?' Shouldn't you do the same thing when you send your money to schools?"

Chapter VIII

MAN, WOMAN AND THE STATE

So God created man in his [own] image, in the image of God created he him; male and female created he them.

—Genesis I: 27

. . . every political theory which does not regard mankind as being what they are, will prove abortive.

—John Jay

The point of my essays was that while admittedly women can do pretty much anything that men can do, and do it pretty much as well, they can also do something which men do not show, and have never shown, any appreciable aptitude for doing; they can civilise a society.

—Albert Jay Nock

This beautiful verse in Genesis makes a statement about life that is central to all that we are and do and hope. Like so many other traditional teachings, it is a matter under furious modern siege. But this one is novel among them in that the enemies of a harmonious order seized the initiative and the high ground without resistance. In other words, we who would defend civilization abdicated our responsibilities and leadership. As a result, our task to put things back into perspective becomes very much harder. But it must be done.

Please savor its hauntingly exquisite expression, a signal of its truth: " . . . God created man in his [own] image, in the image of God created he him; male and female created he them."

Male and female. Two sexes, alike in God's image. *Opposite* sexes, to use a term we have all but forgotten in our latter-day urge to obliterate distinctions. Male and female, neither of which quite understands the other (although the male will often ruefully concede that the female understanding is better). Two complementary sexes, halves of a whole in which both find their fulfillment.

The modernist attack on these rather everyday propositions states that there are not any significant differences between the sexes. Oh, of course, there are a few obvious dissimilarities in our biological functions, particularly in procreation and childbearing. But on the whole, modernist theory states, we are alike; we are not created man and woman but each an indiscriminate person; our roles are interchangeable. In this we abandon all our old concepts of motherhood and fatherhood in favor of unisex parenting. "Parent" as a verb is not new, but the notion that you can be either parent, Mom or Dad, is a modern fantasy. And so, in our delusions, we are presented with a media bombardment about the househusband who stays home nurturing infants while the liberated wife strides man-fully into the work force. The husband is often depicted as a buf-foon, the housewife as a drudge. Only the young woman is invari-ably done glamorously, and only if she acts like a man.

This is indeed fantasy, not only in theory but in fact, as we will see. We entertain too easily the mistaken notions of the radical feminist. As I noted, we (mainly males) have indulged and chuckled about feminism to the point of allowing nonsense to occupy the high ground. What we hear and face now is no innocent matter, like the "war of the sexes" of yesteryear. That was ever a good-humored affair, and nobody expected anything dramatic from it—there was always too much fraternizing with the enemy. Today, what we face is assuredly serious. The modern feminist has learned to be an activist and to seek state intervention on behalf of her theories. Using the coercive power of the state is strong medicine. What she has mainly achieved is directing the wrecking ball toward her own long-term interests, and toward that of men as well. There are fearsome consequences to be paid if we deny our nature.

But this trend was evident long before there was such a thing as a feminist movement, or any feminist expression at all. Its course was the rabid egalitarianism of the left, a dubious ideal that denies both diversity and excellence. Must we, in the name of equality, be reduced to the lowest common denominator? Each of us is unique. We all have our own unique ways and values and dreams. How is it even possible to think of equality, and to give up our individual merit and diversity, save in being equal before the law? Yet the urge for "equality" was, and remains, an overwhelming political influence. Richard Weaver wrote back in 1948, "The most portentous general event of our time is the steady obliteration of those distinctions which create society . . . . And the most insidious idea employed to break down society is an undefined equalitarian-ism."

Elsewhere in the same work, Weaver addressed at length the effect of modern impiety, fueled by the egalitarian muse. Here he speaks of what it does to women; and this was, to repeat, many years before anyone had ever heard of a radical feminist:

> I put forward here an instance which not only is typical of contempt for natural order but which also is of transcendent importance. This is the foolish and destructive notion of the "equality" of the sexes. What but a profound blacking-out of our conception of nature and purpose could have borne this fantasy? Here is a distinction of so basic a character that one might suppose the most frenetic modern would regard it as part of the *donnee* to be respected. What God hath made distinct, let not man confuse! But no, profound differences of this kind seem only a challenge to the busy renova-tors of nature. The rage for equality has so blinded the last hundred years that every effort has been made to obliterate the divergence in role, in conduct, and in dress. It has been assumed, clearly out of this same impiety, that because the mission of women is biological in a broader way, it is less to be admired. Therefore the attempt has been to masculinize women. (Has anyone heard arguments that the male should strive to imitate the female in anything?) A social subversion of the most spectacular kind has resulted. Today, in addition to lost generations, we have a self-pitying, lost sex.

About all that has changed is that things have gotten worse, and that now we do hear arguments, and no end of them, that the male should imitate the female. Weaver is irresistible; let me quote one other comment:

> The anomalous phase of this situation is that the women themselves have not been more concerned to retrieve the mistake. Woman would seem to be the natural ally in any campaign to reverse this trend; in fact, it is alarming to think that her powerfully anchored defenses have not better withstood the tide of demoralization. With her superior closeness to nature, her intuitive realism, her unfailing ability to detect the sophistry in mere intellectuality, how was she ever cozened into the mistake of going modern? Perhaps it was the decay of chivalry in men that proved too much. After the gentleman went, the lady had to go too. No longer protected, the woman now has her career, in which she makes a drab pilgrimage from two-room apartment to job to divorce court.

Where is all this taking us?

"Sexual Suicide"

In 1973, the feminist or "women's liberation" movement was flying high. Books by such prominent feminist authors as Kate Millett and Germaine Greer were almost guaranteed immediate best-seller status. The movement was a special favorite of the media, and its views and theories were aired constantly. For the flavor of these great doings, remember that we were still in the era of the 1960s turmoil: the hippie and flower child "counterculture," and the rampaging New Left anti-war demonstrations and riots and bombings. Anything went, so long as it was left-wing and a slap in the face to traditional American culture and values.

The feminist movement was very much of the left in its thinking, though it had its own essence. We need not summarize its views in any detail. Besides, it spun out so many theories, and changed its line on this or that point so often, that an exact summary at any given moment would be impossible. The gist of it was that the male of the species oppressed the female. The oppression chiefly took the form of forcing her to be *female* in her nature and role in life. It was imposed from birth by her upbringing and training, and throughout life by sexist customs and laws. It made her feel inferior and a slave or sex object. But she could do anything he could, and more, and she could get along without him just fine, thank you. She was fed up with this patriarchy and determined to break its grip, so that she would be free to seek her destiny, wherever it lay. She would be liberated herself from her female nature and roles. She would henceforth be equal in every way, from a respected role in life, to salary, to legal protections.

I trust this is a fair characterization. I am doing the best I can to make it so, albeit from an outsider's position. (I conspicuously am not mentioning the more disputatious theories, like Susan Brownmiller's assertion that all men are rapists, as these may have been put forward just for shock value or sass.) It is not my purpose to call these views into question—yet. On the contrary, I think these are eternal human feelings and wishes, and one can sympathize with them.

Sufficient, for now, that this was a powerful indictment of half the human race, including me. Its power was at flood crest in 1973. To question any of these charges was to invite mud on your face and footprints on your back.

Yet it bothers me, after the fact, that nobody did. My own male reaction at the time was roughly that this was a purely female affair. It was their business, not ours, and if it did them some good, that was fine too. Of course no defense of the male or his role in life was needed. We were confident of ourselves and thought we could get along just fine. Perhaps this reaction is typical; I do not know. What I do know is that the feminist attack had the field largely to itself, and often went unanswered.

One observer looked deeply into the whole matter and said: This is wrong. It will bring us, man and woman alike, to grief. In 1973, George Gilder brought out a book called *Sexual Suicide*. In the teeth of prevailing feminist sentiment, it argued the old wisdom that men and women really are different, and that biology or our sexual nature has everything to do not only with our personal fulfillment in life but with the survival of civilized society. *Cosmopolitan* Editor Helen Gurley Brown had written a book called *You Can Have It All*—meaning marriage *and* career *and* liberation from sex roles. Gilder's book in effect replied: I'm sorry, but no, you can't have it all, any more than men can. That is not the way things are. You will find your fulfillment in being true to your nature as a woman. In this you are sexually superior, and you must use your power to civilize society as you bring into the world, and nurture, new life. . . . In his own words, with a rich lode of contemporary data and experience, George Gilder echoed the old words, " . . . God created man in his [own] image . . . male and female created he them."

Well! All this went straight into the feminist fan, and Mr. Gilder was promptly named "Pig of the Year"—a title he bore with such humor and delight that he retired the trophy. Oddly, the point that made them angriest was that they were *superior* sexually. How dare he suggest that women held the reins in the procreation and betterment of humankind? That would restrict women to their immemorial "role"! But let us note also that a vast number of women, then and now, are not feminists, certainly not in the left-wing movement sense; and among these, many were ecstatic about what Gilder had to say. Here, finally, they said (and I have heard this often), is real understanding of what it means to be a woman. As a man, I am in no position to judge; but Gilder's thesis makes all kinds of sense to me. He developed it by deep and often firsthand study of the single male, from which he gained a new appreciation of female nature and its moral power. Recently, he rewrote the whole book from scratch, using new data (*Men and Marriage*), and even he was surprised at how much his thesis had been vindicated by events unforeseen and unforeseeable in 1973. "I didn't have to *fight* so hard," he said of it. But let us see for ourselves. You decide.

At the heart of things, said Gilder, is that each generation—in every society—suffers what may be called an invasion of barbarians: young men. Single men.* They are, by their in-built nature,

---

*It has since occurred to me that in the invasion of the 1960s, the barbarians finally won. Their influence sucked what was left of humane liberalism into the wacky left. The humane liberals, disaffected, became what we now call neo-conservatives. But the New Left types carry on from the academy, where many are tenured

aggressive and energetic. Where shall they put their boundless energy?

The traditional answer is marriage. Stripped, for a moment, of all uniquely human and spiritual meaning, down to raw biology, the woman is saying: You may have a part in your own long-term future through procreation. But your future passes through my womb. To obtain it, you must agree to provide for me, and for our children, for the rest of our lives.

Of course, this is not a very elevated way of looking at the human condition, but it does put some important things into the right focus. The woman's sexual superiority is obvious, despite feminist protestation. That she bears the children is paramount. The choices of procreation are almost entirely in her hands. That she must (and will) use this power for the betterment of society at large is not so obvious. Still at a biological level, she will choose the best mate she can. But what does this do for America, other than improving its breeding stock?

Gilder's answer is that it turns male energy to productive purpose. Marriage offers him the role of provider and protector, into which he can pour his energy. That this traditional role is very much the right role shows up in all the statistics. The married man is in every way healthier, happier and longer-lived than the single man. Conversely, when marriage ends, the divorced male becomes susceptible, and then some, to all the psychological and physical ills of single men. Which are many.

In other words, a man *needs* this role of provider. He needs in the most basic way the feeling that he is taking care of his family and protecting it. He needs to be attached to a family. It is his link with his own specific, acknowledged children, and thus with his posterity. "Motherhood," said Margaret Mead, "is a biological fact. Fatherhood is a social invention." Indeed, and an invention that is necessary to civilized life. The father's attachment to his children

professors. They are still hooked on group think, analyzing all things in terms of race, class and gender, and they still thump the old Marxist tub. They would not know a human being if they met one. Their influence is baleful, and likely to remain so—unless they get married and grow up. As we shall see.

(which is often not acknowledged in primitive cultures) is an immensely civilizing force. It gives him a moral and long-term perspective in life, where as a single man he had had only a short-term view and no permanent hopes or dreams. Thus a woman's offer in marriage acts to channel a man's energy into moral and productive effort. In a sense she tames him, and she will go on being the moral leader in her home.

These same phenomena, written large, largely dictate the peace and prosperity and moral betterment of society. As Nock had seen many years ago, women are the civilizers, and they do it by converting men to their own long-term, maternal and highly moral view of life, through the instrument of marriage.

Unless male aggressiveness is domesticated and turned to productive purpose in this manner, the whole society is in trouble. On this count, we are in big trouble.

Singles

The single man, especially when he is young, is unable to see much beyond the present. He is disconnected from his future in that he has no children, no family, no part in the greater biological fabric of life. He cannot develop the moral view of his life that encompasses his role as a father. He will seek and find his manhood, if at all, in the streets. In effect, his untamed and amoral aggressiveness will be turned loose against civilized society. He remains a barbarian in our midst. Here, all the statistics tell a grim and uniform story. Young, single males commit practically all the violent crime. Overwhelmingly, they are far more susceptible than married men to emotional and mental disorders, to disease, to homosexuality, to drug and alcohol abuse, and to other patterns of anti-social behavior. All these problems and patterns multiply even more among young men who grow up in a fatherless home—a problem epidemic in the welfare culture, equally among all races. These unfortunates have never had a father's guidance and discipline, nor had a model of the man's duty to provide for his family. They are left confused and full of doubt about their own identity.

I am not, of course, saying that a given young single male is headed for trouble, or that he cannot be productive or civilized. But his far greater susceptibility to many problems holds up only too well as a generality. We have, in the past, regarded the unmarried female as something of a social misfit, and unkindly termed her a spinster or old maid. In truth it is the young unmarried male who is the misfit, and who often takes out his anger and frustrations in anti-social ways.

None of these problems particularly afflict the young single female. Her place is essentially assured by biology. In all cultures, and in practically any sort of home, she will grow up to self-assured womanhood. In no culture does anyone worry that she will not; it is the young male we worry about. Rarely will she have doubts about her sexual identity. Born to motherhood, she is innately closer to the biological nature of life, and she understands it better than the male. This nature, in turn, is the center of moral understanding, which begins with an infant at its mother's breast. Women instinctively recognize the sacred and inviolable value of the newborn life. Men, as a rule, do not; they have to be taught—by women. From this beginning, the woman will maintain the moral directions and leadership of her home. She is fully ready for all of this while still single.

We see, then, that the most fundamental processes of human life and its continuity flow from "man and woman created he them." Perhaps this was all so obvious and settled that we gave scant thought to it when it was called into question by radical feminism. Now we have a great deal more to think about; for the new, chic, liberated role for women popularized by the feminists is a prolific source of unhappiness for both men and women. In its scorn for the immemorial contribution of a wife and mother, it runs against biological fact as well as moral advance. To recall an old advertising line, "It's not nice to fool Mother Nature." Nature tolerates no such disorder. She will exact the full price of our folly, to the last penny. This is what we now see in terms of personal unhappiness and social disorder. More disturbing, the foundations of civilized life are being eroded; for society depends on young women turning men to productive and moral purpose.

Of particular concern to me as an educator: One side-effect of
this confusion of roles is the near-total eradication of all-male and
all-female colleges. There is nothing at all wrong with coeducation.
Hillsdale College has been coed since its very first class in 1844,
and we are proud of it. But Hillsdale was the exception. In earlier
times, most colleges were for men or women only, just as they were
all private and religious. One must respect the wisdom that created
them so. I am certain that we lose something deep in education by
catering to the unisex murmurings of our times and abandoning
traditional ways.

Liberation from What?

What is it that a feminist, liberated from her role as a woman, wants
to be? She wants to be a man. That is, she wants to do the things
men do, work out of the home as a man does, earn the same money
men do, enjoy all the respect and prestige of men's activities, join
the formerly all-male club, and so on. It is interesting that the thrust
of feminism is ever to be masculine. The movement employs the
force of law as much as it can to give women traditionally male
status. Examples are civil rights and anti-discrimination statutes
based on sex, equal pay provisions, and Affirmative Action, which
demands the hiring of women and minorities despite less qualifica-
tions for the job. (Apartheid in South Africa similarly protects Afri-
kaaners' jobs and status, although with more stringent laws; do we
approve of that?)

On the drawing board are "comparable worth" laws and tax-
financed day care centers. "Comparable worth" would have the
bureaucracy—rather than the market—decide what jobs are worth,
in order to give women equal pay. This is an atrocious idea, not
only for the bureaucratic morass it promises, but because it is as
anti-female a scheme as one could devise. Insofar as bureaucrats set
their pay over market rates, women lose jobs and opportunity. Several prominent feminists agree: "Dumb and dopey," says Susan
Brownmiller. Federally funded day care centers are another assault
on marriage and the home, and a brutally expensive one. Lost in all

this frenzy of do-goodery is what it means for a woman to try to be a man—a thing by nature she cannot be.

Society, says George Gilder, depends on having two sexes. Each must be true to its nature. The two sexes are not alike, but rather, are complementary. The two sexes are inherently unequal as well, and no amount of wishful thinking will change the fact. A man may beget children throughout his entire life. But a woman has a limited and much shorter period of her life in which she can bear children. These roles and their implications are necessarily different. Which is not to say that one sex or the other is "superior," a very foolish matter to debate. Just different. Most of us hugely enjoy the difference!

Among the implications is that a male has a biological interest in taking the childbearing powers of more than one woman. He would, if permitted by law and custom, keep a harem, and such things are indeed done in some cultures. In our own life we see this happen when a man divorces his wife and marries his young secretary. Whatever else may be involved, underneath is the biological fact that the man can still beget children later in life and that he has an instinctive urge to do so. But, says Gilder, this instinct must be tamed by monogamous marriage. Cultures where it is left unchecked do not and cannot rise to the level of civilization. They never solve the problem of channeling male aggressiveness and energy into peaceful and productive work, and thereby lose capacity to adapt, create and progress.

Life and especially monogamous marriage are a great deal more than biology, of course. Marriage can create a spiritual balance between man and woman that is attainable in no other way. Such balance is strongly stressed in the Christian concept that man and woman are unfulfilled halves until united as one flesh in matrimony. This balance is all-important in rearing children successfully, in two ways. Where the mother and father are secure in their complementary roles, children rarely have any difficulty finding their own rightful identities, whether male or female. Second, in the shelter of both parents' long-term commitment, love and moral instruction, they grow up secure and morally self-controlling. Perhaps one need only say: they grow up. Society at large has an enormous stake in the healthy, moral development of new generations within the intact family. We learn late, and to our peril, that there is no substitute for it. As we see in our discussion of families elsewhere, single-parent households, despite honorable exceptions, do a relatively poor job of raising children. They lack the needed balance. Their children grow up confused and prone to trouble; how will they, in their turn, raise children well? The female-headed household has especial difficulty bringing up boys. The girls will usually turn out fine, but the boys have a terrible time finding their manhood. If they don't seek it in the streets they may well look to the fiercely paternalistic religions like Islam, or to aggressive male political causes and such "models" as Lenin, Che Guevara or Hitler.

Here we get to the crux of our latter-day dilemma. All the ideological forces of our time conspire against the conventional woman's role and marriage. Young women are urged to renounce that role and be free. They are counseled to be assertive and pursue careers, to marry later if they marry at all, and defer childbearing. They are endlessly portrayed in the media striking masculine postures in masculine activities, and looking *tres chic* in pants and sports cars and karate studios. They are told to join the rough and tumble of politics and get involved in "the movement." They are especially urged to be sexually liberated, use contraceptives, and have sexual relations purely for their own pleasure (but make him use a condom). Even so seemingly small a matter as using the word "Ms." helps destroy a critical distinction, and adds to their confusion. To bolster their liberation, practically all laws and social sanctions against promiscuity have been torn down. We are awash in pornography. The media fairly drip with sex. Cohabitation is routine. Casual sex is approved. Divorce has been liberalized, in both law and custom, to the point of destroying our concept of permanent marriage. Alimony laws have been repealed. Oh yes, you've come a long way, baby. But are you better and happier than you were? Or are you acting out a radical fantasy designed to cut you off from your roots and fulfillment in life, and thrust you, helpless and dependent, before the almighty State?

Clearly, all these factors and forces are working against traditional marriage, and they are potent. Let us be clear. No one says marriage is the right thing or the only option for every woman. No one denies any woman the right to pursue a career if she wishes to; it's a free country. But one ought to say, as George Gilder does, that if you make this choice, you risk great unhappiness in your life. In trying to be a man, or to do the things a man does, you may forfeit your fulfillment as a woman.

More particularly, we come back to that unyielding fact that a woman has only so many childbearing years. If she spends them pursuing a career, as her feminist sisters urge, they are gone—irretrievably. If she even defers marriage for a while, she will find herself running out of time and chances. And more: she will have that much less time and chance to know her own grandchildren—especially while she is still young and able to enjoy it to the utmost, as a woman will. Similarly, if she succumbs to the blandishments of "sexual liberation," she is giving away her sexual bargaining power. She will get nothing in return, except, perhaps, an unwanted pregnancy or venereal disease. It is the male who is liberated and the female who pays most of the price. Sexual liberation is expensive. As the coarse old saying had it, why pay if you can get it free? If she expects a commitment or even gratitude, she will be disappointed. She has by her own choice liberated the male from marital obligations; in reality from being a man. And in the larger sense, both he and she are much poorer for it. She has thrown away her support and security in marriage and all the fulfillment it entails, and is now forced to earn her own support in the rat race. She has also thrown away a much more reasonable and fulfilling career choice: simply to pursue it after raising her family. She lives longer than a man and can look forward to many years for her career. The man has been gratified in his short-term outlook and sexual drive, but equally loses his long-term moral male outlook and his fulfillment as father and provider.

Multiply these circumstances and civilized society begins to suffer and even disintegrate. This is exactly what Gilder meant by the term sexual suicide, and he specifically applied it to the whole of society. The young male remains untamed; his energies and aggressions are often turned against society. One result is a more than doubled prison population since these allegedly "liberating" notions have been in vogue. Another is the spread of AIDS. Instead of adding to the general welfare (the capital pool, if you wish) he subtracts from it. Concurrently, the young woman's natural ability to enforce moral behavior by the male is thwarted. This is even more serious, for civilization can exist only on the basis of our shared understanding of what is right and wrong. It is not as easy to find statistical measures of the women's frustrations in this new regime, but there are some. For one, in many studies, their constant complaint is that men are not manly enough; by which they mean men are not as responsible, mature, morally steadfast and confident in their masculinity as they used to be. This complaint can fairly be directed to their feminist sisters, who gutted the masculine role even as they tried to emulate it. In the process, they cut the bonds that bring men into moral harness. It seems that if a woman wants man to be a man, she had better be feminine rather than feminist. Even more to the point, perhaps, men and women alike had better remember that "male and female created he them," and seek our destiny jointly in what we really are. To do less is, indeed, the destruction of society by sexual suicide.

I often talk about leadership. In what we discuss here, women are or should be the leaders we so urgently need. These matters come as close to the basic human condition as we can get, and are, I think, more important than all the masculine concerns put together. They are not alone about home and family and children and happiness, but about peaceful society and the very continuity of human life. They are, in short, the matters that have always been safely entrusted to women. For a woman to lead in them, she need only be, proudly and confidently, herself.

Postscript

Where man and woman alike lose, who can possibly gain? The political left *thinks* it does. It knows that normal relations between man and woman, and the families they create, both moral in nature, are fierce bulwarks against the dreamy utopian schemes it would like to impose upon us. Therefore it seeks to destroy both, and it does so with a silky, siren call to be *really* free, beyond any natural or moral limits. Forget what you are, it croons; despise the moral law (it is just your inhibitions); be promiscuous; be free . . . . Sounds good, doesn't it? I myself yield to no one in devotion to genuine liberty, but this has nothing to do with liberty. It is a scam. It is a scheme to destroy what means most to us, and to make us dependent upon the state.

Of particular interest to women, I trust, is that this scam intends to yank them out of their home and into the work force—so that they too can pay taxes to support the dreamers. This has already happened in Europe. In Sweden, as recently as 1965, Allan Carlson reports, 75 percent of mothers with children were full-time homemakers. Now, 90 percent of them are working. Not coincidentally, in the same period, divorce rates soared, as did "cohabitation" rates, and now living alone has become the norm. The birth rate has fallen far below "zero population growth," as it has in almost every developed country with some sort of social security, including America. This, in turn, results in a spiral of accelerating economic decline. America has escaped the trend so far largely through immigration and the influx of "illegal" aliens. Carlson writes, "This is, of course, the fulfillment of that two-century-old statist vision of man, alone and naked, at the feet of a gentle Leviathan." But the left wins nothing; it only destroys.

The real winner, and the only winner in all this, is the not-so-gentle Leviathan, the state. It is the state that feeds on our disputes, especially those between man and women. It is the state that fattens (one wonders how it could grow any fatter, but it does) from busybody legislation promising, but never able to deliver, "equality." It feasts on our every departure from moral behavior. Wouldn't it be easier (not to mention cheaper) for us to love one another, and to behave?

Chapter IX

MORALITY IN THE MARKETPLACE

But if any provide not for his own, and specially for those of his own house, he hath denied the faith, and is worse than an infidel.

—Paul; I Timothy 5:8

Gain all you can. Save all you can. Give all you can.

—John Wesley, founder of Methodism

Economical: Managing, or managed, with frugality; avoiding waste; frugal; thrifty; saving. . . .

—*Webster's New International Dictionary,* Second Edition

This will be yet another discussion of our vanishing moral values, but from a probably unfamiliar perspective: free market economics. I am going to argue, in the teeth of modern thought, that the market is not only efficient, which everybody concedes, but is erected on a moral foundation, which will bring a shriek from any liberal or socialist soul listening in. Let them listen harder. I will go further. I argue that the market is efficient *because* it is moral, and that socialist experiments invariably fail (and they all certainly do) because they are fundamentally immoral.

From my view, both sides of the great modern debate make a mistake when it comes to economics. Those of us who believe in a divine order to life and in human liberty are ready to defend the moral law in every instance: except the marketplace. The market is our conceit. We hold the patent on economic science. We developed, honed and tested the correct theories. We know what works, we know why it works and why socialist theories do not work. With few exceptions among us, that is how we defend free market economics: it works. Not: it is morally right, but: it is more efficient. Well, of course it is more efficient and everyone knows it, including the leaders of the Soviet Union. But why are we using a pragmatic rather than moral argument in *this one* case? Why do we say, knowingly, that the market is propelled by self-interest? That translates into greed, and the socialists stuff it down our throats. I don't blame them. We have it coming for not looking more deeply into our own position and finding its moral basis.

All "systems," capitalist or socialist alike, are based on self-interest, because all creatures have self-interest. "Greed," if you want to call it that, is no free-market monopoly, any more than concern about others is the exclusive property of liberals; it is more nearly the other way around. But we forget, self-interest encompasses spiritual ends as well as material. The question we should ask, and too seldom do, is: Which system channels human interests and energies to their highest moral ends?

Modern statism makes the same error in reverse. Socialists and kin believe in a materialistic and amoral reality, yet their whole economic case is moral. They say that private property is unjust and business profits evil. This is a lingering prejudice going back to some atrocious economic theorizing by Karl Marx himself in the nineteenth century. It is nonsense. But give them due credit. They know enough to make a moral case. It has been the collectivist stock in trade for a century. In its way, this is a refutation of their most fundamental belief in a godless, natural world that has no room for moral man. Yet, moral men we are, and to our heart and sense of justice they appeal. The socialists err in turning timeless moral law upside-down. They reached that point via blunders in economic theory.

Morality and Markets

Every economic question raises moral issues, which it is my interest to explore. The economics cannot be changed. Market activity is ruled by iron law. When we interfere with supply and demand, say, we may not know exactly what will follow, but we know it will be unpleasant. We seem to have no such respect for the moral law. Our standards of morality can be, and often are, bent for personal or ideological purposes. There is always an *economic* price to pay for this too, and we all pay it. This is needless waste: it defeats both our personal wish and national policy to help the poor and needy among us. Where we fail is precisely in not understanding the moral nature of economics. Perhaps we err in putting lowly, mundane commerce in one mental pigeonhole, and our moral and spiritual aspirations in another, and saying to ourselves, the economic and the divine cannot have anything to do with each other. But they have everything to do with each other. This we must recognize.

Imagine, at the outset, a society that strictly adhered to the Ten Commandments. Obviously it would be very different from ours morally, but I think it would also be far more economically efficient than we are. The Commandments, after all, begin by talking about God but end up talking about economics. They lay down rules that have direct and important economic consequences. For example, the prohibitions of murder, stealing and lying would eliminate crime, including any sort of fraud in the market. One can think of scores of ways this would reduce costs and enhance efficiency—not to mention the relief of getting to and from work without fear of being mugged. The Commandments to honor our father and mother, and not to commit adultery, strengthen the bastion of productive activity: the family. Property rights are given divine sanction in the Eighth and Tenth Commandments, which prohibit stealing or coveting what belongs to others. There can be no such thing as a free market without private property. All laws and taxes that infringe property rights—we have a ton of both in this country—are harmful to the economy. Thus, strict adherence to just these two Commandments would go miles toward a truly free and efficient market. But it would do far more than that! It would remove social-

ism and all the related "isms" from our vocabulary forever. Central
to every brand of socialism is the belief that private property is evil.
Either God or Marx is wrong on the point; believe whom you will.
For economics, it is no contest. God's law bears good fruit, and
even Marxists (if any remain outside of backwater despotisms and
certain American universities) have long since given up on Marx.
Following the same two Commandments in this country would remove welfarism from uncaring government bureaus and restore it
to the private citizenry, where the impulse to help resides and where
the job has always been done best.

We could go on and on. What ever would the liberal media
do, for instance, to fill up their news slot, if they could not stir up
and feature fashionable "victim" groups coveting someone else's
money? How could the story of socialism ever have been told had
it not turned covetousness into a fine art? Its whole recruiting message is: This little bee is getting too much honey so that one isn't
getting enough, so he should resent it and join the cause. Socialism
is organized envy. Whatever may be said for this in terms of morals
(nothing), it is hopeless economics. Everything about its statement
is economic nonsense. In the end envy can be mobilized to steal,
but not to produce, and that is the immemorial road to hunger. But,
we needn't go on imagining how things would be if we really
obeyed the Commandments. The point of the exercise is to show
how closely moral law and economic law are entwined. In fact, if
we repeated the thought experiment by imagining living in a really
free market, we would get essentially the same results—because
we would be following the same rules.

Traditional moral teachings, especially the New Testament,
are full of economics. In the story of the young man troubled by
great possessions, Jesus says, "*Sell* whatsoever thou hast and give
to the poor if you would be perfect." Why not just give it to them
outright? Because, then as now, the possessions were not money
but lands, herds, vineyards, buildings. The poor have no need of
such things, but rather, need food and clothes and tools, or a little
cash to buy them. As writer William Rickenbacker pointed out
some time ago, there must have been wealthy buyers, then as now,
and a market must have existed for capital goods, with which Jesus

was familiar. "How hardly shall they that *trust in* riches enter into the kingdom of God," He cried, speaking of the young man (emphasis added). Yet He could not have assumed that other wealthy people would damage their souls by buying the young man's great possessions; would He have corrupted them? The Good Samaritan could handle his wealth, the young man could not. Possessions are neutral, neither good nor bad. The danger of wealth, so vividly illustrated in this story, is that we may end up trusting it instead of God. But in another sense and in another story, we cannot be like the Good Samaritan ourselves unless we have the economic means to help.* The moral question is what *we* are and what we do with whatever wealth we may have. Money, even great riches, are in themselves just . . . stuff.

In the Parable of the Talents, Jesus metaphorically likens investment, usury and money changing to making the most of what is given us by God, while He scorches the servant who buried his money hoping to please his master by giving it back intact. None of these metaphors need cause discomfort; we still have markets for, roughly, stocks, bonds and foreign exchange. And it remains true that the eccentric who buries his coins does nothing for anyone else. Indeed, the only way the rich can harm the poor in a *free* marketplace is to stuff their money into the mattress. If they spend it, which is usual, they create jobs. If they put it out at interest, the market will allocate it efficiently. They may invest it on their own: if wisely (and it does happen at times), they help us all, but if poorly, they surrender their capital to someone who will use it better, again to general benefit. It is only the nonuse of our gifts, or our capital, that ultimately harms. The lesson in economics is again much the same as the lesson in morals. Similarly, in the Parable of the Laborers in the Vineyard, Jesus affirms the sanctity of contract and, implicitly, of property rights. The lessons are there for us, if we will but heed them.

Our whole Judeo-Christian heritage differs from the mystical

---

*Margaret Thatcher argues that it is morally outrageous to promise aid to the needy without having the means to do so; which is about all liberals do. I agree.

East in conceiving us to be, as it were, part beast, part angel, with hungers of both body and spirit. We are instructed to tend both sides of our nature, and to do it well; to be ready at need to abandon the worldly for the spiritual, but not to go overboard about it. In miraculously feeding the multitudes in the desert, Jesus had the most practical concern: "I will not send them away fasting, lest they faint in the way." So, too, we must feed body and soul alike; or, we could say, nourish the economic as well as the sacred. In both we are moral agents, given the great gift of choosing between right and wrong. Economics, after many earlier and lesser definitions having to do with wealth or commerce or the like, finally becomes the science of choice.

Real economics acknowledges, and is concerned with, all our choices, not just those in the world of business, the intangible along with the tangible. (This too we owe to Mises, who called his work praxeology—the study of all human action.) As value-free science, economics has nothing whatever to say about the moral value of our choices. Rather, it studies the results of what we choose or might choose. But it can say, and does, that there will be consequences to every choice, moral choices very much included, if only by default. We cannot do everything at once. Were you to sit on a mountain and never touch money again, this would still have analyzable economic results: the rat race minus one, perhaps. But it is you and I who make the choices, and when we do, our moral values are always at work.

William Rickenbacker writes:

> The great glory of economic thought is that it steps aside at this point and allows the transcendental part of human existence to come fully into play. Economics, properly conceived, always makes room for such highly individual choices as charity, abstinence, poverty, or in the purer language of earlier times love, purity, humility. In Russia it has been a crime to choose one of these values rather than to produce widgets for the state. It is the common failing of totalitarianism from Pharaoh to Gorbachev that it attempts vainly to deny that there are always certain people who will not be satisfied with merely material agglutination.

Individual choice is what makes the free market free and efficient, and what gives us all the hope to make the best of what we
have been given. That hope is taken away from us when moral
teachings are perverted by ideologues who serve the state instead
of God. The growth of government, spurred by a failure of moral
responsibility, has been the principal story of modern times. It is a
dismal, blood-soaked story, now at last coming to an end. Whether
we understand it and use our coming opportunity to reclaim our lost
freedom and moral leadership remains an open question.

Morality According to Karl Marx

The biggest political story of our times is this: socialism is dying.
When we analyze this earthshaking event, we usually get no further
than remembering socialism's economic failures and political oppressions. These offer reason enough, surely, to be glad at its passing. But are they sufficient to bring down a system that has been
oppressive and an economic failure for most of this century? I think
not. Surely the roots of the socialist decline go much deeper. Until
we understand the causes, we will not be unable to heal the frightful
wounds socialism leaves behind, and indeed, we will ourselves
remain in peril of repeating the same mistakes.

The most striking feature of this final decline of socialism is
that it is *not* accompanied by the triumph of capitalism. You would
expect a dozen books and a thousand articles proclaiming victory
for the free market. You would expect a massive defense and explanation of capitalist ideas—and perhaps some crowing about how
much better they are. You would expect conservatives, especially,
to redouble their efforts to expand liberty. There are some articles,
a few books, but there is no concerted effort to claim victory, and
the fight for freedom seems to be dying out. The near-silence is
ominous. It is as if we had achieved great ends with evil means and
ought to be ashamed rather than exultant at our success. But this
guilty feeling is itself a socialist hangover. We should be rid of it
once and for all, or Marx will have the last laugh. We should be
delighted with free market performance for all the right reasons.

As I have been saying, it is capitalism that has the proper moral credentials.

The economic performance of socialism is dismal everywhere it is tried. It cannot compete with the free markets of the free world. We leave it in the dust. But it is not economic failure that is killing socialism. We would be greatly mistaken if we assumed that all that people in the socialist countries want is more consumer goods. Certainly they would like more and better food, housing, clothes and appliances—wouldn't we all? But it is not a yearning for mere possessions that moves them. After all, they have from the beginning endured economic disaster, shortages and shoddy goods, yet felt their system was better.

The death of socialism is spiritual failure. The triumph of "capitalism" is equally a spiritual victory, although we do not yet recognize it as such. I put "capitalism" in quotes because it is a Marxist coinage and a hate word. It is bad coinage—all systems are necessarily capitalist, because they all have to allocate capital. But everyone is pretty much agreed about its Marxist and principal meaning: a free market system based on the ownership of private property and the free exchange of goods. I am happy to accept this meaning and insofar as I use the term, that is what I mean by it.

When I say capitalist ideas are better, I mean precisely in their spiritual dimension. Of course they are more efficient; everybody knows that. It is hardly worth saying. What few see is their moral goodness. We are still blinded by that awful bit of Marxian theory I have mentioned—called the labor theory of surplus value—that stood moral law on its head. The theory disappeared from formal economics by 1870 (even the socialists found it an embarrassment), but its false conclusion is still with us. It is summarized by an economic encyclopedia (which mentioned the "notoriety" Marx gave it) as follows: "Profit is unpaid labor appropriated by capitalists as a consequence of the institution of private property."

In other words, according to Marx, the capitalist system, and it alone, causes poverty (by paying low wages), unemployment and periodic depressions. Private property is bad, profits (also rent and interest) are stolen from workers, and capitalists are all greedy, grasping, mean and exploitive. And so they have been portrayed for more than a century of Marxist propaganda. By extension, wealth is considered ill-gotten and tainted, and many a rich person has financed revolutionary causes out of guilt for earning or inheriting wealth. We need only document real cases of nasty capitalists and exploited workers (there are plenty)—ignoring everything else—to make the case seem valid. But it is nonsense, and the evidence against it, in both theory and fact, is overwhelming.

Notice two things. This theory is the perfect *excuse* for every personal failure in the market. With it you can blame anything on the capitalist (the boss, your foreman, society, the system). You didn't succeed because you were being exploited and stolen from. It is human nature to want to excuse one's own mistakes, and here Marx offers absolution for any failing, free for the asking. You don't even have to repent. But there is a price: to believe it you have to learn to hate. This is the second thing to notice. The "bourgeoisie" (or "ruling class") and the "intelligentsia" (educated people) are to the communist dictators what Jewry was to Hitler: the hate object against which to "unite the people." Totalitarianism requires a permanent enemy, a group to hate. The hate object must be an abstract class (individuals are too concrete and too well known to each other), and it must be "evil." Once a would-be dictator persuades you to hate this class, you are his slave. He is in complete control. You even stop thinking for yourself. It is only a short step beyond this to justify or to take part in genocide—the Gulag or the Holocaust. The genocidal oppressions that always follow the establishment of socialist states are not "betrayals of the revolution" (the standard true believer's excuse), but the logical culmination of immoral socialist ideas.

The important thing is not that Marx butchered economics in the nineteenth century, but that he drew quasi-moral conclusions from his hapless theory. It is little remembered now, but Marx first advertised his theories as more economically efficient. They got nowhere. In fact they were drubbed by experience: capitalism was booming and wages were rising rapidly when Marx published his predictions that workers would be reduced to poverty. Only when they lost the argument about efficiency did the socialists turn to a moral argument, saying that capitalism was unjust. Only then did they prevail, for there was no rebuttal in moral terms. The claims of capitalist evils have been the whole strength of socialism ever since, and still pollute such intellectual swamps as Beijing, Ethiopia and a number of American campuses.

But capitalism is not unjust, as we have discussed above, nor even amoral; its structure and rules are as ethical as they are efficient. It is socialism that is unnatural and immoral, as is finally becoming clear after the cruelest century in human experience. The hatred and envy it innately appeals to are sins to a Christian, and a bad thing by any ethical reckoning. Free markets, in contrast, not only appeal to our moral instinct to help others, but harness our energies to that purpose, and reward most those who do the most for humanity.

Morality in Econ 101

All of us live in a whirl of activity that involves the transfer of goods and services. We sell our labor and produce, or rent and invest our capital, for money. With our money we buy our food, clothing, shelter and the niceties of life. There are only two ways goods can be transferred. The first is one-sided and involuntary to one of the parties: One party takes what the other has, without giving anything of value for it. This is called stealing, or taxes. (In fact, that is the government's own definition of taxes. We may get something of value for the tax, but it is not obliged to give us anything, and what we get, if anything, need not be something we personally value.) Obviously, in such a one-sided transfer, the first party gains and the second party loses. It may look like a break-even transaction or "zero sum game" in the larger scheme of things, but it is not; as we will see, it reduces the value of the goods to both parties, and is thus a net loss to the country. It also directs future behavior by both parties to less productive channels, adding to the net loss.

The second is two-sided: both parties voluntarily agree to the exchange. Its key feature is that it is freely chosen. This kind, and this only, may be called an economic exchange; the word exchange even implies the consent and approval of both. When we see *why* both parties agree, we have the key to the whole of modern economic science. It is simply human nature. Each of us is one of a kind, not only in mind and body, but in our talents, wants and goals. We each have a unique scale of values for what we want, how much we want it, what we will do to get it, and so on. Moreover, our wants and goals change constantly: we want food when we are hungry, not right after a meal. We each know what is the best thing to do according to our particular needs at a given moment, and we act on our self-knowledge; nobody else knows, and nobody else can decide for us. No two of us ever have quite the same scale of values directing what we do.* You can easily see this at a well-stocked cafeteria: rarely will two people choose exactly the same meal. The differences between us are, as the saying goes, what make horse races—and the whole free market. We make all exchanges because we value things differently. You exchange your dollar for the loaf of bread because you value the bread more than the dollar. The baker agrees to the exchange because he values the bread less than the dollar. Such is the nature of all exchanges in the market, no matter how complicated they may seem in their details. It is invariably a matter of two (or more) people trading something they value less for something they value more.

The principles we derive from this fact are so important that they figuratively make the world go round. First, both parties *gain* from the exchange, each according to his own scale of values. This alone refutes the pre-Adam Smith (1776) notion that there is only so much wealth to go around, and therefore if somebody gets some of it, he has to take it away from somebody else. What hogwash! Wealth is constantly being produced and consumed. It is distributed through the marketplace. The more of it there is, the easier it gets for all of us to have some: that is simple supply and demand. Marx, who thought he was a student of Adam Smith, managed to restore

---

*What this discussion puts forward, in everyday terms, is the Subjective Theory of Value, the foundation of market or "Austrian School" economics. Many superb economists have contributed to it, but none more, I believe, than Ludwig von Mises (1881–1973), whose library is preserved at Hillsdale College.

the same old hogwash with the claim that capitalists *steal* their profits from workers. But in fact, both worker and capitalist gain as they themselves see it in the employment of one by the other; both give more to each other than would be available in alternative situations; both get richer. In economic terms, one man's gain anywhere is everyone's gain, everywhere. We rightly applaud every economic advance, and lament every loss, no matter where in the world, and in doing so build human sympathy and brotherhood.

Second, and here we get into subtler effects, the goods or services exchanged increase in value, because both parties value them more highly. Or, you can say that they move from less to more valuable usage: more efficient allocation. Free exchanges, therefore, are a constant process of moving goods, capital and labor to where they are most useful, and making us all richer in the bargain. The opposite is true of one-sided exchanges. The thief who steals your special new car values it much less than you do, and will dump it to a fence for a fraction of its value to you. Easy come, easy go. But you, who worked hard to get that car, will feel burned and unwilling to invest so much of your energy next time. What good would it do if somebody can just come along and steal all your effort? To both of you, the car loses value, and the world is that much poorer.

The third principle, just spelled out, is incentive. When we make a good exchange and are rewarded for it, we have much more motive to do it again. Reward for our effort brings out our best in the market. Contrarily, when we are cheated out of what we earn or own by crime or taxes, we lose interest in working so hard. Every dollar of our taxes is a disincentive to economic production. Where state exactions become extreme, as in socialist countries, work gets sluggish and sloppy, and the workers turn to booze.

Final Thoughts

Someday we will have to learn anew that the government is the larger part of our problems, not the answer to them. America was founded in a rebellion against the kind of do-good government we have now (only a lot less of it). Once we knew better: government cannot do good for us because it has no resources of its own to do good with. It cannot give to one what it does not first take from another. The taking is fundamentally unjust—a denial of your basic right to the fruits of your labor. Liberals can think of a thousand and one reasons why somebody else *needs* your money. So can a six-year-old. That does not change the fact that it is your money. You earned it. If you want to give some of it to the needy—and Americans are the most generous people on earth—that is your right and no one else's.

It is when we forget these fundamentals that we get into big trouble. We institutionalize covetousness. We institutionalize confiscatory taxation to pay for the "good" we do. From a moral view, this is reprehensible. From an economic view, it makes no more sense than everyone stealing from his neighbor. Indeed, in economic terms, that is exactly what we are doing. If we steal instead of produce, how will we eat? How long will it be until we, like the Russians, have to stand in line half the day hoping to buy some poor sausage?

Our half-century-long reversion to Old World statism has brought us to this: Today, one dollar in every three we produce is confiscated from those who earned it and is given to those who have no right to it. One dollar in three. We are still a wealthy people, but no nation can survive forever so great and systematic an assault on its ability and incentive to produce. If our moral sense no longer tells us this, our gift for economics should. Every dollar we confiscate is devalued. The so-called transfer makes it worth less to both the taker and the taken. At the same time, every confiscation is a disincentive to future production. When our earnings are taken away, we have less reason to earn and we will do less tomorrow.

The worst part of the whole tax-thy-neighbor system is that it is so addictive—it feeds on itself. When much of our money is taxed away, we feel cheated and lose all our moral qualms about getting to the trough ourselves, one way or another, to get it back. That's only fair, isn't it? I understand perfectly, but no, it isn't. All we are doing is resorting to the same bad means that cheated us in the first place. It is precisely this that gives overweening government its strongest hold on us. But two wrongs still do not make a right. Someday we must learn to say no to what is not ours, even if we have been cheated.

On a national scale, I do not have any answers for this unholy addiction to other people's money. From a historical view, it is a fatal disease that has brought down many a rich and proud civilization before us. On a personal level, the answer could not be more obvious. Just say no. Let us be the cheated, if it comes to that, but not the cheaters. It is we who must lead and who must do what needs doing. Nobody else can, least of all the government. It's that simple.

Chapter X

TAXES vs. THE MARKET

Then all the elders of Israel gathered themselves together, and came to Samuel unto Ramah,

And said unto him, Behold, thou art old, and thy sons walk not in thy ways: now make us a king to judge us like all the nations.

But the thing displeased Samuel, when they said, Give us a king to judge us. And Samuel prayed unto the Lord.

And the Lord said unto Samuel, Hearken unto the voice of the people in all that they say unto thee; for they have not rejected thee, but they have rejected me, that I should not reign over them. They have forsaken me, and served other gods, so do they also unto you.

Now hearken unto their voice: howbeit yet protest solemnly unto them and shew them the manner of the king that shall reign over them.

And Samuel told all the words of the Lord unto the people that asked of him a king.

And he said, This will be the manner of the king that shall reign over you: He will take your sons, and appoint them for himself, for his chariots, and to be his horsemen; and some shall run before his chariots.

And he will appoint him captains over thousands, and captains over fifties; and will set them to ear his ground, and to reap his harvest, and to make his instruments of war, and instruments of his chariots.

And he will take your daughters to be confectionaries, and to be cooks, and to be bakers.

And he will take your fields, and your vineyards, even the best of them, and give them to his servants.

And he will take your menservants, and your maidservants, and your goodliest young men, and your asses, and put them to his work.

He will take the tenth of your sheep, and ye shall be his servants.

And ye shall cry out in that day because of your king which ye shall have chosen you; and the Lord will not hear you in that day.

—I Samuel 8:4–18

Noah must have taken into the ark two taxes, one male and one female. And they did multiply bountifully!

—Will Rogers

An income tax form is like a laundry list. Either way you lose your shirt.

—Fred Allen

There are two classes of people who dislike paying income taxes: men and women.

—Anonymous

Somebody in prehistoric times invented government and thereby added "taxes" to "death" as tribulations* mankind could not avoid. It is hardly clear that we are better off for it.

Anthropological research has shown that government grew out of conquest; especially the conquest of peaceful settlements by nomadic warrior tribes. The nomads learned that slaughtering a farm village for its meager possessions is much less profitable than enslaving it and *taxing* it. This meant that a few of the nomads had to settle among the villagers to keep an eye on them and pretend to look busy. Presumably once a year at harvest time they extracted their tribute at spearpoint, skewering a few malcontents who resisted or cheated on their form 1040. Later, the rulers learned to pose as gods, settle local squabbles and hand out favors, to make the system look better and keep their subjects in line. They also invented writing and bookkeeping to record their deeds and tax rates, which was the beginning of history. But the system remains essentially unchanged, as Nock gleefully reminded us in *Our Enemy, the State*. It is still almost always imposed by conquest. It is still in the tribute business, although nowadays we have more so-

---

*Incidentally, the word *tribulation* (suffering, oppression) is derived from Latin and French roots meaning to extract tribute; to tax excessively. Governments do a lot of that.

phisticated words for it, such as "bracket creep" and "revenue enhancement" and "tax reform."

The Old Testament had, if possible, an even sterner view about governments and their "kings," namely, that they were punishments for sin. I quoted the whole story at the beginning of the chapter because it is probably no longer familiar. It is worth reading with care. For one thing, the Israelites, the chosen children of the Lord, did not have a government until the event described. Imagine! We automatically assume that this is the worst thing that can happen and will result in chaos. But here were the chosen people living without a state for centuries. The children of Israel eventually lost faith in the Lord, and said to Samuel, "Make us a king" to lead us in war and to judge us, like other nations. They chose human authority rather than divine, and in doing so, chose their own servitude—which seems to me also the principal story of modern times. The Lord said to Samuel, tell them the price they will pay; not that it will do any good. Samuel told them: you will be mercilessly taxed. Your money and land and property and servants and even your own children will be appropriated for the grandeur of the king. And you will cry out in that day, because the Lord will hear you no more. But the Israelites paid no attention, and gave up their freedom to have a king.

This is, I grant, pretty far from modern political theories and from what we usually think about government. But the trouble is, we *don't* think about the nature of government. Its actions affect us daily and we think a lot about those, but its underlying nature is as invisible to us as water is to a fish. We accept it as something we are born into, that is there, that has always been there, that will always be there. This mute and unquestioning acceptance is a victory for the state and all its pretensions. It is equally a defeat for our own forefathers in America who regarded the state, at best, as a necessary evil, and who fought for independence from big government. We, like the Israelites of old, have strayed from the paths of liberty, and are paying dearly for it in lost freedom and burdensome taxes. In this perhaps more than in any other case, we learn that we have to make things happen by ourselves. To turn over all of our complaints and problems to the government is to give government the power to destroy us. Personal initiative and responsibility are the only answers.

The feature of the state that makes it different from all other human institutions is that it employs coercion and force. It enforces its will through compulsion, and it has the armed power to do so. No private organization of any sort may use coercion. No corporation can compel you to buy its services as government can. In the private world, all things are done by free choice and persuasion. Should we use violence or the threat of violence to get our way, it is a crime. The state has a monopoly on the use or threat of force, and this gives it an enormous advantage in its dealings. It need not compete for revenue or favor, it need not cooperate as others must, because it can compel. This advantage is subject to endless abuse and throughout history has been endlessly abused. The people in government, after all, are ordinary humans as susceptible to temptation as anyone else; and they face far more temptations than the rest of us! Can we be surprised that they succumb to the corrupting influence of power? In the last analysis, the only protection we have against political oppression is the limited size, and therefore relative weakness of the state. The form of a government does not matter nearly as much as the amount of power it wields. Invariably, the bigger the government gets, the bossier it gets, and the more it acts like every other big authoritarian government. That we, the people, are ourselves supposed to *be* the government in republican theory* does not change this fact one bit. We have all of human history to tell us that force and violence are very dangerous intruders into human affairs. State compulsion is the opposite of liberty; take it from an expert: "It is nonsense to make any pretense of reconciling the state and liberty," said the founder of the modern communist state, Lenin. Of course it is.

The actions of the state raise many moral issues that we ought to talk more about, but in fact discuss less and less. *Are* government

---

*This is a lovely idea, but it only works with a weak, limited, constitutional government. When government gets the power to do more or less anything it wishes, we can no longer control it and become subjects instead of citizens. Police and other officials commonly *call* us subjects now.

efforts to "do good" morally impeccable? Or are there serious and legitimate moral objections to these practices? Such discussion as there is—an incessant drone in the media—is always concerned with the benefits of state action and pleas for ever more benefits. But it rarely pays much heed to the costs. I think the moral issue *begins* with the costs, for government has no wealth to do good with, nor any means to produce wealth, for that matter. It is also in debt up to its ears, or rather, up to *our* ears, for we and our children must repay what it borrows. In a word, it can only take. It cannot give what it does not first tax away from us. In taking, it does what is immoral according to the Eighth Commandment and illegal when anybody else does it, except that it's legal and all right and just the thing we need more of, some say, when we call it taxes. "Taxation is theft," said Proudhon, who was apparently unable to distinguish as well as we do between the street-corner variety and form 1040. Not to stretch things too far, government is a parasite.

Taxes, descended from tribute exacted by ancient conquerors, remain the lifeblood of the state. Taxes are thus an excellent proxy for the moral questions concerning the state, and also a near-perfect index of how much government we are forced to put up with. Of course, modern rulers are much too sophisticated to boast of their power over their enslaved people, as they used to (when it was obvious to everyone anyway). Slave systems are out these days and Robin Hood is in. But I'll bet that if forcible taxation were seriously challenged—in favor, say, of voluntary contributions to state welfare—the conqueror of old would reemerge at once, and we would again find ourselves the property of the state. For that, to the level that we are taxed, is exactly what we are. Nothing makes this clearer than the income tax and its sneaky, no-deduction, soak-the-poor, add-on twin, the social security tax (which is also an income tax and which in many cases takes more than the 1040).

The moral issue could hardly be much simpler. Where justice says you are entitled to the fruits of your labor, the income tax takes a large and unearned cut for the state, by force. Where justice says, "To each his own," Treasury says, "Oh, no you don't—we get ours first." Where the Lord tried to terrify wayward Israelites with the specter of a 10 percent tax rate, the modern state knows no limits to its exactions. England, I believe, once set the income tax rate at over 100 percent: which is like saying, we'll take everything you earn *and* you must send us the family silver. Nothing so severe has ever happened in this country; our top rate was only 96 percent. Fortunately(?), thirty years later, we learned of the Laffer Curve and its argument that if tax rates are too high, taxes are a disincentive. Production will fall and the taxes on production will also fall, so there will be less money for the state. Of course. The supply-siders won the argument, for which we may all be grateful, but they also handed the state a tool for fine-tuning tax rates to "generate" more money by reducing rates. Here, in short, is the way to feed the most possible money to the government for its accustomed purposes of bungles, botches, boo-boos, blunders, boondoggles, bloat, bureaucracy and butchery. Is this really a good idea?

No. Morally, our case is that we are not the property or "subjects" of the state, that we are born free and have basic rights to our freedom and property, and that the state's denial of these basic rights is immoral. Let us look at some cases. There is more to learn, for immoral means lead to immoral results. Not idly is it said that the power to tax is the power to destroy.

The "Monstrosity"

What do you suppose the *New York Times* called "a vicious, inequitable, unpopular, impolitic and socialistic scheme . . . the most unreasoning and most un-American movement in the politics of the last quarter-century"? What did the *Washington Post* call an "abhorrent and calamitous monstrosity" that repudiates "the spirit as well as the letter of Democracy"? The answer to both questions is the income tax.

This was an early version, passed in 1894. Its rate was one percent on incomes over $4,000. This first peacetime income tax affected only one person in one hundred (the standard of living was lower then, and the dollar was worth much more). By the following summer it had been challenged all the way to the Supreme Court and had been declared unconstitutional. And good riddance. "We have seen the end of attempts to tax income," crowed the *Times*. "This is still a land where honest men cannot be made to pay tribute to schemes, drones and dupes," opined the *Post*.

Tell us another! The tax wiggled back on the federal agenda within fifteen years. In those few years, Fabian socialism was being heavily imported from Europe and had become the new "cause" on campus. The Progressive Era stirred up many new demands to tax, spend and meddle. The federal deficit reached an alarming $89 million (about one two-thousandth of latter-day levels). By 1909 an income tax amendment was drafted and sent to the states for ratification. Proponents said the tax would *never ever* go above five percent, and would be imposed on only a few people, those best able to pay. The *Times* opposed it, with perfect insight: "When men get the habit of helping themselves to the property of others, they are not easily cured of it." But the *Post* switched sides and endorsed the tax—to reduce the deficit (a favorite excuse for taxes to this day, and one that invariably increases the deficit).

After the Sixteenth Amendment passed in 1913 and an income tax was imposed, the *Times* got in one last shot, using a biblical metaphor. The tax, it said, is a "rock of credit from which abundant streams of revenue will flow whenever Congress chooses to smite it. We may be sure that it will be smitten hard and always harder, until the national conscience, if there is such a thing, revolts against the inequality and injustice of such a plan of taxation."*

The national conscience remains notably silent on the matter to this day. Its one-time voices, the *Post* and the *Times* and many others, have given decades of their finest thinking to the search for more and better smiting.

You cannot give politicians visitation rights to your wallet and expect them to say, politely, "No, thank you." Anyone could have guessed that our take-home pay would suffer, but perhaps not how much it would suffer. It is a depressing subject, but we'd better have a quick look at the whole wretched mess. That first tax in 1913

---

*Echoing Alan Sherman's pun, I wonder if we are *ever* going to "give up smoting"?

was one percent on incomes over $3,000 (or $4,000 for married couples). This was still a good deal of money and fewer than one person in thirty-five was affected. Indeed, only one banker and lawyer in five earned that much. The tax was progressive with a top rate of seven percent on high incomes, belying its proponents' promises not ever, ever to go over five percent. It actually peaked at 96 percent in World War II, although this rate affected very few.

With the exception of the First World War years, the income tax remained largely an assault on a few highly productive, high-income earners, and did not raise any great amount of money. As late as 1941, the take was $41 million. But massive inflation—itself a tax—in the Second World War years drove up nominal incomes, so more and more workers had to pay the income tax. The burden on incomes of $5,000 quadrupled from 1939 to 1947. In the years since, economic growth and more inflation made the income tax a general tax that almost every worker must pay. It even taxes teen-agers in their part-time minimum-wage jobs. Moreover, inflation pushed even modest incomes into progressive rates once meant to "soak the rich," and at the same time eroded the value of exemptions for raising children. In the Nixon-Ford-Carter years, in case we have forgotten, the politicians *loved* deficits, which were supposed to "stimulate the economy." One excuse is as good as another for pols, who have to spend everything they could borrow as well as everything they could tax, and then turned the red ink into inflation to spend some more, driving up effective tax rates in the process. If ever there was heaven on earth for real, red-blooded politicians, this was it. The hogs did wallow.

A tax-feeding frenzy like this sends false economic signals in every direction, taking vast sums of money out of productive invest-ment and putting them into faulty speculations. This can destroy the whole economy in a hurry, and in the instance, very nearly did. The Misery Index (inflation plus unemployment) rose to over 20 per-cent. Interest rates (real interest plus anticipated inflation) got so high that the huge real estate business was stopped dead. Inflated prices for farmland led to massive and unwise speculation that in due course all but wrecked the family farm. Many other industries suffered similarly. Another result was the lingering Third World "debt crisis," from unsound loans made when inflation was running riot. We were lucky to escape the whole situation with three years of depression (or recession as it is now called). Depressions are not random events but corrections of previous monetary chaos caused by government mismanagement—and greed.

One other feature of the income tax must be mentioned: tax withholding. This was a World War II invention, just when the income tax was beginning to bite everyone hard. It is, in my opinion, the single worst facet of American government, and the one most responsible for Washington's wasteful, drunken-sailor spending. Its "good" feature, that we feel little pain in being taxed, is exactly what is wrong with it. We don't feel the pain and we should. We don't know how much we are paying. If we did, you could hear the screams all the way to Mars, and I suspect our long experiment with do-everything government would be over by the next afternoon. Meanwhile, tax withholding keeps money pouring into politicians' hands, which is like giving cocaine to a drug addict. We cannot hope to have responsible government until we shut off its supply of easy money. The repeal of tax withholding would do that in one stroke.

Other Taxing Tales

Item. Traveling the byways of England, you can see many old houses with only one or two windows, and may find even older ones bricked up tight, with no windows at all. The English do not like to live in gloom any more than we do. So why didn't they have windows? If you find this puzzling, you did not reckon on a window tax.

A *window* tax? If that seems ridiculous, you obviously do not understand the niceties of state thinking, nor do you reckon on so thoroughly progressive a fellow as King William III, who reigned from 1689 to 1702. Here is the story. Before his reign, the coins of the realm were crude, hand-hammered pieces of irregular size and weight. If you got a perfectly round one of the right weight, it was sheer luck. This will not do at all; commerce all but ceases if one coin is worth $1.00 and the next is worth 91 cents. It was common for citizens to clip the coins: that is, pare tiny bits of precious silver and gold off the edges. For some reason, the crown did not regard this as a high-minded effort to make the coins rounder or to equalize their value! The penalty for anyone caught in the act was death—hanging for men, burning for women; and it was often imposed. If you were caught merely possessing shavings from coins, the penalty was being branded on the cheek with a red hot iron. But you could escape the punishment by turning in two other people supposedly guilty of the same. Of course a lot of people got turned in, guilty or not, and my guess is that few of them were friends of the coin clippers.

King William's brilliant idea for solving this mess was a new coinage. The coins would be machine-made, with fluted edges to deter clipping. But he foresaw that they would not circulate until the old ones were withdrawn*: people would hoard the new, more valuable pieces and spend the old ones, keeping them in circulation. So, he brightly proposed that the old be traded in for the new at face value. He did not foresee what happened next: coin clipping turned into an epidemic. People raced to shave as much gold and silver from the old coins as they could before turning them in. The value of the old coinage was reduced so much that the government, in the end, could not afford to trade new coins for old. It had to finance the new coinage by other means, namely the window tax, which was imposed in 1695.

From the state's point of view anyway, the nice thing about a window tax is, it is so easy to do. The assessor just counts the windows and says, "Pay up or else." And there you are. If this subjects people to great discomfort and all sorts of health hazards, it is of scant concern to the state. People rushed to board up their houses. But they had to have some light and air, so most kept a few windows and the taxes on those paid for the new coinage in two or three years.

------

*English monarchs had been well instructed on the point by Sir Thomas Gresham, an advisor to Queen Elizabeth a century or so earlier. This is "Gresham's Law," but the idea is much older.

One thing ever to keep in mind about taxes, especially new and innocent-sounding ones, is that they are nearly impossible to get rid of. The window tax darkened England for one hundred and fifty years.*

Item. At the time of the 1988 Olympics, it was noted that the strongest tennis team in the world could have been fielded by *Monaco*—a principality smaller than New York's Central Park. It could have starred Boris Becker and Mats Wilander, both among the top three or four players in the world. England would have been a good bet for the silver, fielding Stefan Edberg, Anders Jarryd and Henri Leconte.

There is something amiss here, but what? Becker, of course, is West German. Leconte is French. Wilander, Edberg, and Jarryd are Swedish. They were all living in self-exile for the same reason: confiscatory tax rates in their home countries. In Sweden, the marginal tax rate on incomes over $34,000 (pocket change for a tennis pro) was 75 percent. In West Germany, it was 56 percent on income over $72,000. Edberg, Jarryd and Leconte chose to live in London after the top rates there were reduced from 60 percent to 40 percent. But Monaco had an even better offer. Declared residents who were neither French nor Monagesque were exempt from both income taxes and capital gains taxes. It had and still attracts an unusual number of highly paid movie stars, musicians and athletes in its tiny population.

That excessive taxes stifle productivity everyone knows. It is not so well-known that in the electronic age, when capital can be shifted around the world in seconds, governments must compete for productive people. Those that offer the lowest tax rates and the most freedom win. Those that remain greedy and keep tax rates too high lose some of their smartest and most talented people. Monaco's economy is booming. Others' loss is Monaco's gain.

---

*I wonder if the Frenchman Frederic Bastiat had this bizarre experience in mind when he wrote his famous fable about the candlemakers who petitioned the government to outlaw the sun because it was unfair competition.

Item. You pay a luxury ("excise") tax every time you use your telephone. Maybe you didn't know a phone is a luxury, but it was after a fashion in 1914 when this "temporary" war tax was first imposed. Today the tax is regressive and uneconomic, but that is no problem for congressmen whose only rule of taxation is "all the traffic will bear." The tax was repealed twice in its first decade, but was reinstated both times. It has had the death sentence imposed sixteen times and survived them all. It is still with us, still "temporary," and just got raised. Do you think this means World War I is about to break out again?

* * *

Item. Barely one-half of our public high school seniors can tell whether 87 percent of 10 is more than 10, equal to 10, or less than 10. This has been put forward as another education horror story, which it is. But one can think of it in another way. Insofar as public education works to socialize our kids and to disarm them from all resistance to the state, you can call it a huge success. Certainly high schoolers who cannot understand simple percentages will be no match for tax-happy politicians.

* * *

I relate these matters as a short sampling of the long list of strange things that happen when the government interferes in the economy. The results may not always be this bizarre, but they are always counterproductive and often highly destructive. The principal interference is taxation itself, and we must ever keep in mind that all taxes come out of the only source of wealth that we have: the private economy. Taxes make us collectively poorer. But the case is much more than this. Taxes subtract more from productivity because they are a disincentive wherever they are applied. Whatever we tax—be it jobs, goods, capital or property—we get less of. Whatever we tax is also reduced in value; jobs, for instance, pay less and are less attractive because of the income tax. The disincentive effect makes it impossible to "redistribute" income without economic damage. It is not an even trade or "zero sum" game, as some claim. If we tax an earner to give to a nonearner, *both* have less incentive to be productive. Thus in all cases taxation distorts normal, productive economic activity, not to mention individual behavior, and distorts it for the worse. Where the burden becomes great, people have that much more incentive to avoid the taxes, and the costs of doing so subtract even further from productive effort in many ways. As in the case of the tennis pros, some of the most productive may be driven out of the country, and they take their productivity with them. But the converse of all these points is also true: when we reduce taxes, we increase incomes, increase property values, increase capital return, and increase incentives for productivity in general. We get collectively richer, and in this, everybody benefits.

Add one detail. I read somewhere that there are more than eighty thousand governments at large in this country. I do not know if this figure is correct (and there is something spooky about not knowing exactly how many governments we are ruled by), but that is an awful lot of hands in our pockets. Every state, county and town in America, every public school district, every sewer district, is a government. What we do know is that all of this governing takes more than one dollar out of every three we earn. Its haul, more than a trillion and a half dollars a year, simply dwarfs any other economic factor, and all of it is taken out of the economy. The numbers are far too large to comprehend. That is too much governing by a very large factor. In fact, I govern myself and do it tolerably well, as does everyone I know, and I'm sure you do, too. Who wants or needs 80,000 governments trying to do it for us?

This kind of taxation is wrong, and it creates our problems instead of solving them. Without it, we would have immensely more time, energy, incentive and resources for both economic and charitable efforts. We could and would overcome our difficulties by ourselves, which is the only way to do it.

Chapter XI

THE FAILURE OF FREE INSTITUTIONS

Throughout our history, we have looked to free institutions for our defense against despotism. At America's founding, the national watchword was liberty. The Founders were deeply worried about the age-old tendency of government to grow until it became tyrannical and beyond popular control. They did not want this grim history repeated here. In establishing a federal government the Founders divided its powers and pitted the interests of each branch against the others so that no branch could dominate—the system of "checks and balances." They limited its powers to a few specific functions spelled out in a written Constitution. It is a measure of how seriously our forefathers took their liberty that these revolutionary protections were not enough to persuade a skeptical citizenry to adopt the Constitution. Still further protections were demanded.

In the first ten amendments to the Constitution—the Bill of Rights—many important rights were guaranteed: freedom of religion, free speech, free assembly, the right to petition for redress of grievances, freedom of the press, due process of law, security from unreasonable searches and seizures, the right to bear arms, and many more. And in case anyone had doubts about it, the Ninth Amendment also guaranteed rights that hadn't been listed earlier, and the Tenth Amendment reserved powers not specifically delegated to the central government to the states and to the people. With the adoption of the Bill of Rights, the federal Constitution was finally ratified—after a struggle.

Looking back on the rights and freedoms guaranteed in the Bill of Rights, they may seem to us more violated than honored. Especially tattered is the federal promise to stick to its specified powers, in the Ninth and Tenth Amendments. It is, nevertheless, interesting to see how farsighted our forefathers were in demanding the protections of the Bill of Rights. What they saw and recited were the ancient abuses of governmental power. Read the other side of the coin: government control of speech, press, assembly; disarmament of the populace, lest it endanger the state; denial of all legal rights in the face of the wishes of the state. All of this adds up to a sort of "Bill of Wrongs" that is the trademark of totalitarian states in our own century. While we ourselves have not gone nearly that far, we have certainly been infected with the thinking of the omnipotent state. And we have little to be proud of, for letting the great experiment in liberty slip as much as it has.

The main reason we have not fallen further is that we still take the Bill of Rights very seriously. Or more precisely, some of it. We sometimes take it to grotesque extremes: as in giving tax-exempt status to covens of witches in the name of freedom of religion or sanctioning the burning of the flag as "symbolic" speech. We sometimes go clean off the pier, as in finding a constitutional right to kill unborn babies, or to fund blasphemy (such as a figurine of Jesus Christ immersed in urine—in the name of "art") with tax dollars. Your money and mine! Despite unspeakable abuses like these, we do well to resist attacks on our genuine rights, whether in the direction of libertinism or despotism.

Even the Bill of Rights did not adequately guarantee our liberty in the Founders' eyes. They theorized that protection of freedom, with as much or even more force than the Constitution, lay in the eternal vigilance of free, private institutions. They meant the Bill of Rights, in part, to guard and strengthen such institutions as a free press, churches, schools and colleges, and charities. These in turn would tame government by continuously exposing corruption and presenting the truth. A free press would keep watch over government and its abuses. A free pulpit would instruct the people in their duties. (All freedom would be lost, the *Federalist Papers* warned, if the citizenry did not remain virtuous.) Academic freedom would transmit civilized values and thus defend against the tyranny of state-directed views. It is an attractive theory, but where do we really stand?

I ask you: Do the media today either fight the good fight for liberty or represent those who do? Do the clergy stick to their immemorial task of saving our souls, one at a time? Do our scholars and professors use their academic freedom to defend the heritage of America and the values of Western civilization? Let us investigate.

The Media Elite

To conservatives, demonstrating a liberal bias in the media is like saying water flows downhill. The slant in the news is there to read and hear every day. It is gratingly obvious to those who are not attuned to liberal cadences. If a news story or broadcast were to take a conservative slant, its bias would be just as obvious to the liberal listener.

Distortion of the news is a serious matter in a country like ours that practices self-government. Citizens must be informed about public affairs to elect responsible officials and encourage appropriate policies. When the citizenry is given weighted, one-sided and otherwise biased information, the very policies of the nation are in turn distorted and warped. They can no longer even be said to represent the "consent of the governed." Rather, they are the result of a fraud imposed on the nation by a small, but powerful ideological elite.

Conservatives maintain that in recent decades the primary news media have been strongly dominated by liberals, and that their reportage is slanted to promote liberal policies. This was plain as early as the presidential race by Barry Goldwater in 1964, or perhaps a few years earlier, as conservative views began to command serious public support.* This state of affairs was to a degree hidden at the time, and arguably less important, because liberal views were then in a majority. But liberalism has been in retreat ever since, culminating in decisive electoral rebukes in all the presidential elections of the 1980s. Liberals are now the minority and do not represent the American public. In fact, their views are so tattered as to be jeered as the "L-word." When the elite use their media power today to tailor the news to liberal specifications, it is like using trickery to regain what they lost fair and square in the elections. It is undemocratic and unfair.

Two other important trends developed about the same time. For one, liberalism moved left. Its traditional emphases on economic freedom, personal responsibility and a limited role for government were already fighting for their lives in the 1930s and vanished altogether in the turbulent 1960s. Similarly, such ideals as a color-blind society gave way to racial quotas and Affirmative Action. It even became reactionary (according to its own earlier definitions) and turned hostile to economic growth, to industry, to development, to science. In other words, in all but name, liberalism became a breed of what is called democratic socialism in other countries. We ought to recognize it as such, in pious memory of an older liberalism that really stood for liberty. One reason that modern conservatism made such huge strides so swiftly is that it filled the libertarian void left when liberalism gave itself body and soul to the state. Today it is conservatives who fight for free trade, limited government, and the rights and responsibilities of the individual.

The second trend was that journalism changed. You might say that it turned left too. This was called adversary journalism or the New Journalism. The whole conception changed, from reporting just the facts, as a service in our system of self-government, to

---

*As late as 1950, Lionel Trilling could say with some justice that liberalism was not just the dominant intellectual view in America but the *only* one. Insofar as this was true, a "liberal press" was the mainstream, and complaints of bias were idle. But that near-consensus was soon shattered by the publication of *The Conservative Mind* by Russell Kirk in 1953, and had ebbed to a minority by 1980 or earlier.

advocacy: using journalism to take sides, and, indeed, taking the side that wants to destroy self-government. The new journalism makes news an ideological weapon. It selects the facts it wants, and twists or ignores other facts that do not fit its ends. If it doesn't have the facts it wants, it turns novelistic and makes them up. In one famous example, a *Washington Post* reporter named Janet Cooke was slated for a Pulitzer Prize (a liberal plum) until some editor thought to check her story about a little boy addicted to heroin. Oops! No little addict. She fabricated the whole thing. The New Journalism also invented news as a "media event." It actually creates news with its own bias in the form of demonstrations and protests and ideological street theater, knowing that the public will be watching on television. Another propagandistic method it uses to the fullest is weighted labels. Political opponents are given ideological labels most of the time ("arch-conservative," "far right"); political friends do not get labeled, to leave the impression they are in the mainstream and objective. We took a dimmer view of such techniques when they were practiced, expertly, by Paul Joseph Goebbels, the master propagandist for Hitler Germany. His official job, incidentally, was Minister of Popular Enlightenment.

Ministers of popular enlightenment, in just the same sense—those are our New Journalists today. But they've added one more trick even Goebbels didn't think of, dubbed "disco Journalism" by a journalist of the old school. The disco reporters are making heroes of everything that crawls out from under a rock, makes hideous noises, splatters paint around, takes off its clothes in public, urinates on crucifixes, invents a new sexual perversion (with bonus points for spreading exotic diseases), or manages in some other way to offend the sensibilities and moral standards of anyone above a goat. It is, to be sure, awfully hard to think of any standards left unviolated. Compose ditties to Satan? Bite the heads off small animals? Masturbate on stage? All that's been done. It's passe. Our need of stronger wine and scummier "heroes" never ends, and our disco newsmen are on duty to create both. If you can think of any behavior that is still outrageous enough to furrow the brow of a shockproofed American, we'll be seeing you on *Lifestyles of the Rich and Famous*.

The destruction of standards is another liberal-left weapon. Remember? They are going to "build a new world on the ashes of the old," and the business still at hand is turning civilization to ashes. It will be interesting to see how the hypothetical New Socialist Man builds a world of finer, more sensitive, more equal and just standards, after arguing that all standards are nonsense and exterminating those who disagree. Perhaps a new and greater civilization will rise in which children, starting at age six, are required to bite the heads of small animals.

Meanwhile, for those of us who prefer civilized life to the jungle, the media's distortion of information for political ends, and their concurrent assault on moral values, pose a very nasty threat. But we have some ways to fight back. The first is to know we are in a fight. The second is to tell the truth. It is up to us to expose the liberal-left bias of the media elite, and so to make them be more objective. Beyond that, we should take a larger part in the media ourselves, through ownership when that is possible, or at least through some truth-telling in the op-ed columns and letters sections.

Let's be clear about one thing, though. It is natural to be partisan in one's views, whether liberal or conservative or some other view. In free America, it is your right to hold any view you wish. The apparent question is whether a news reporter or editor should be perfectly objective, despite his personal views. My answer may surprise you. No, he need not and should not. But he must be fair and provide a balanced view. And that is what we have been missing in the news—fairness and balance.

Let me explain that I am a historian. It is not desirable, or even possible, to write up any bit of history as a recitation of straight facts. You need to make it a story, and you need some larger story—for instance, the settlement of the New World, or the opening of the American west by pioneers—to fit in your piece of history. The larger story is mythic (my prior readers know I do not use that word in any derogatory sense). It necessarily will involve goals and moral values as well as facts. History is a story in the full human dimension. We like to think the pioneers, crossing the prairies in Conestoga wagons, were good folk fulfilling a good American impulse; and that, in the sense of myth, is true. They *were* good people, establishing a church and a school at every crossroads settlement. You could venture many an objection, say, about their greed for California gold or their harsh treatment of American Indians, without undoing the overriding myth or story.

Exactly the same considerations apply to journalism. It is not possible to be perfectly objective, nor is it desirable. News too must fit into a story, a view of life. Barebones facts, with no interpretation or explanation, mean nothing, and are of no interest to us. Journalists must refer to the big picture, which, in the case of news with some degree of political content, means political ideologies. There are vastly more "facts" each day than time to report them as relevant news. Therefore reporters tend to select the facts that are congenial to their ideological view. We cannot object to this per se. But we can and do object when they become advocates and choose, shade, twist or ignore the facts to make a political case. That goes beyond the bounds of balance and truth. It is mere ax-grinding. And it is an insult to any claim of providing fair information. That is what is wrong with advocacy journalism.

Are the first-source media* controlled by liberals? Even they admit as much. If you don't want to take their own word for it, there have been a number of quality studies devoted to the question, all with the same answer. Yes, they do. Do they slant the news in their own favor? This they usually, but not always, deny. Yes, they say, the media are dominated by liberals, but no, that doesn't influence their work. In that they are either badly mistaken or trying to feed us a line.

There are several think tanks and research centers devoted solely to keeping track of liberal bias in the media. I am familiar

---

*The main news-gathering organizations, sometimes called the "media elite," are generally agreed to be: the *New York Times*, the *Washington Post*, and the *Wall Street Journal*, among the major newspapers; *Time* and *Newsweek;* the three television networks, ABC, CBS and NBC; and the two main wire services, UPI and AP. Some lists also include the *Los Angeles Times*, *U.S. News and World Report* and Cable News Network (CNN). Of all these media, only the *Wall Street Journal*, and then only on its *editorial page*, is conservative (the *Journal*'s reportorial staff is notoriously liberal).

with two publications which do the same, and there are probably more. They monitor media newscasts and count up every pro and con statement. They count the minutes of favorable versus unfavorable coverage of political issues. They give you graphs and statistics. They survey the use of ideological labels, which can be done in detail, very easily, by computer. Books have been written since the late 1960s plotting the same sort of material, full of statistics. I have in front of me as I write a dozen studies demonstrating liberal media bias. More accumulate every day. I could throw twenty pages of it at you here and now, some of which has real shock value. But I'll spare you most of it, settling for an example or two. For instance, Edith Efron simply counted the number of words used by network news people concerning certain key issues in the 1968 presidential election. For Richard Nixon (this was long before Watergate), the count was: 860 words for; 7,493 words against. Note how unbalanced this is, particularly in an election that Nixon won. A similar study checked media "spin" (bias) in the 1984 election, in which Ronald Reagan was a landslide victor over Walter Mondale. The spin against Reagan, measured in news seconds, was about ten to one: good press, 730 seconds; bad press, 7,230 seconds. For George Bush (then the vice presidential candidate) the spin was 1,510 seconds of bad press, and *no* good press at all. The Democratic candidates, Mondale and Ferraro, both got more good press than bad—which is pretty hard for anyone to do in the press, and harder for politicians. Press coverage was not only unbalanced but hostile to the views of the electorate.

Another discovery by *MediaWatch* was heavy traffic by news people into political jobs and back again (called the Revolving Door). Nearly four times as many liberals as conservatives hop in and out of political beds. Now, nobody supposes a job at, say, the Democratic National Committee is going to be nonpartisan and objective. Is it so easy to suppress your views in the one job and shout them from the rooftop in the other? Or are liberals' views present in a news job as well as a political position? Finally, there is the simple fact that virtually all complaints about media bias are made by conservatives. You *know* the liberals would be screaming if conservatives were in charge of the media and slanting the news.

(Who has ever been able to shut them up on a matter they found unjust?) Their silence is eloquent testimony of who's inflicting ideological bias.

Here is one last example, in detail. The media have their own "philanthropies," and it is interesting indeed to see where their money flows. According to its president, the decision of the New York Times Company Foundation "to make grants is guided entirely by indications of the usefulness and effectiveness of the applicants and not by ideological considerations." Strange, then, that the Times Foundation made grants to more liberal-left groups than any other media foundation and managed to channel 96.5 percent of such funds ($436,000) to them. Two conservative groups received a total $16,000 in the same period (1982–86) or 3.5 percent. (*MediaWatch* dug out the figures and prepared the report.) Here is the money passed out "not by ideological considerations":

Grants	Organization (liberal)
$10,000	American Friends Service Committee
$19,000	Aspen Institute for Humanistic Studies
$29,000	Brookings Institution
$10,000	Children's Defense Fund
$ 9,000	Conservation Foundation
$20,000	Council on Foreign Relations
$25,000	Environmental Action Coalition
$21,000	Environmental Defense Fund
$15,000	Environmental Law Institute
$15,000	Feminist Press, Inc.
$28,000	Foreign Policy Association
$ 3,000	Government Accountability Project
$ 3,000	King Center for Nonviolent Social Change
$45,000	NAACP
$ 5,000	NAACP Legal Defense and Education Fund
$ 8,000	National Audubon Society
$ 5,000	National Commission on U.S.-China Relations
$20,000	National Public Radio
$20,000	National Urban League

$ 6,000	National Wildlife Federation
$ 5,000	The Nation Institute
$11,500	National Resources Defense Council
$19,000	NOW Legal Defense and Education Fund
$24,500	Planned Parenthood
$12,000	Population Resource Center
$10,000	Sierra Club
$ 5,000	Urban Institute
$24,000	Wilderness Society
$ 5,000	World Resources Institute
$ 4,000	World Wildlife Fund
	(conservative)
$10,000	American Enterprise Institute
$ 6,000	Media Institute

Similar patterns of donations were reported for other prominent media foundations, including those established by the Times Mirror Company (*Los Angeles Times, Baltimore Sun, Newsday*), Philip L. Graham (the *Washington Post, Newsweek*), General Electric (owner of NBC), and Capital Cities (ABC and a number of newspapers). The General Electric Foundation was "the least one-sided"—only about three-to-one liberal—donating 27.6 percent of its grants to conservative groups, as opposed to 72.4 percent for liberal groups.

* * *

The result of every study, survey and poll is the same. It is just what we started with and see everyday—there is a strong liberal bias in the news. If you want a profile, the media elite are overwhelmingly white male, from comfortable families preponderantly in the Northeast. They have much more education than most of us, make a lot of money, care practically nothing for religion, vote almost unfailingly Democratic, for the left-most candidate, and are more liberal or leftist than most Americans by a wide margin. They are not main-street Americans and do not represent the political norms.

Make what you will of the demographics. What catches my eye as an educator is the level of "education" (55% of the elite made it to graduate school). Liberals love to boast that they are better educated and therefore smarter than the rest of us. They aren't and they aren't. But one thing they can boast is spending a lot more time in the classes of the leftist professoriat at "prestige" universities. It would seem they have learned their lessons well.

A real pity these newsmen-to-be didn't come to Hillsdale. We play fair.

From Charity to the Marxist Social Agenda

I hope this statement shocks you: *Americans are far and away too generous.*

How can I say this? Generosity is a good thing. Rightly do we take a fierce pride in our compassion toward the handicapped, the sick, the needy and the disadvantaged. Indeed, we are adamant that generous provision be made for almost anyone who can plausibly present himself as a "victim" of almost anything, including his own self-destructive behavior.

But the old saying, "generous to a fault," has real meaning, and in our times, the faults have multiplied into catastrophes. For example, in our "compassion" for the poor, we have doomed the so-called underclass, millions of people, to a life of dependency and despair. The "War on Poverty" has trapped them not only in permanent poverty, but in a dehumanized existence that wrenches families apart, foments violence and drug abuse on the streets, and makes their escape to a good life prohibitively expensive. As we look deeper into the question, we will find that Christian charity has, over a long period, been subverted into an engine to impose on us the Marxist vision of society—often by force. If this succeeds, we can say good-bye to our generosity. We will all be needy.

Of course it is not our charitable impulse that is at fault. It is the means by which our generosity is distributed, and, more recently, many of the ends to which they are given. We no longer discriminate between worthy causes and those that at times are actually harmful. The main problem is, giving has become impersonal. We no longer take personal responsibility for our gifts, save for a few group or church or local functions. Mostly our donations flow to large institutions that we think are "philanthropic"; but are they?

Or worse, we accede to the government's siren song to take care of problems for us—which is not charitable at all on our part. *You* and *I* can, perhaps, afford the extra taxes to pay for this (and for all the waste and bungling that is inevitably involved), but a vast number of people cannot. There is many a family of modest means who pay their way in life but who must watch every dime in the grocery store. Our careless resort to tax-paid "compassion" adds greatly to their burdens and at times impoverishes them. When we do not take responsibility for our wish to do good, we actually create poverty, instead of alleviating it. But never mind, for now, the infinite problems of government "welfare." These are well known, universally acknowledged and widely discussed.

We are concerned here with the private (at least to the extent of being tax-exempt) and huge "philanthropic" industry. This includes foundations, churches, trust funds and the like. It is institutional in nature, and, if we include voluntary labor, is estimated to run to $500 billion a year. That is a big business indeed; crudely, one approaching half the trillion-dollar-plus federal government budget. What do we know about it? The honest answer for most of us would be, nothing at all. Did you know, for instance, that when you put money in the collection plate at church, some of it is likely to end up in the hands of communist terrorists in Africa or revolutionaries in Central America? Or that, even by making an innocent purchase from a large corporation, you are probably helping to finance radical feminists, gay and lesbian groups, left-wing think tanks and other radical causes?

Yes, activities like these are very much a part of what we call "philanthropy" or "charity." In truth, they are a large part of that half-trillion-dollar "philanthropic" industry. In our ignorance of what this vast enterprise really does, and in our abandonment of our own responsibilities, we accept at face value that all this is a good thing. It is if you are a believer in the liberal-left dream. For those of us who share the older American vision of a free and moral life, and who would never knowingly contribute to radical causes, this is a wake-up call! Our own money is financing our destruction. But we don't have to put up with it, so long as we know what is going on.

My own ignorance of the problem got a swift kick at a recent meeting of a scholarly group of which I am a member. I had heard rumbles and warnings before, but this particular meeting really fixed the focus, and dug into the whole matter. On hand were experts on four fronts. First, the veterans of an unknown, silent fight to maintain a true moral dimension to "do-good" enterprises. Second, investigators who have poured over corporate records to discover how often huge corporations are sloshing money to left-wing causes, without an apparent thought that they are slitting their own throats by doing so. Third, theoreticians, particularly of "public choice" theory, who show us why our good intentions and "compassion" so easily—all but inevitably—come to grief. Fourth, representatives of a pathetic handful of trusts or foundations which still uphold the genuinely charitable impulse and the free-market orientation of their founders.

Of the last group, it should be noted that all foundations were originally endowed by their founders' success in the market. But it turns out that it is nearly impossible for the founder to insure that his fortune will be used for either market-oriented activity or other good purposes he intended. After he or she dies, the money will perforce be managed by others, who will use it for their own agenda. And that, in all too many cases, is liberal and statist. The founders' genuinely decent purposes are as a rule distorted and often are turned upside-down. Only in a handful of cases has the philanthropist been so far-sighted as to see this coming, and therefore establish ironclad rules to make sure his fortune is used as he wished. The few who succeeded in protecting their beneficence were nearly all represented at the meeting I referred too—in *one* panel discussion.

In any case, it is true, and true in far greater scope than we realize, that the foundation world is under the leftist thumb, and is used to finance leftist activities without number. The story behind this perversion of values is very long—going back more than a century. I will make it short. It runs parallel to the broader trends of secularization and socialism that I discuss elsewhere.

Recall how things were a century and a half ago. The young Republic was robust and libertarian. There was no welfarism, no dole, no income tax. There was virtually no federal presence at all. People were on their own, to succeed or fail as they might. Did the multitudes starve? Did they go uneducated? Of course not. Hillsdale College was founded at this time, by Free Will Baptists. That was how things got done: through dedication and true charitable impulse. In fact, every college in America had been founded by religious groups. In the case of Hillsdale, the impulse dictated that our college would be open to all, from the first, regardless of race or sex. It was set up in a shabby, abandoned store, and its only teacher was a spanking fresh college graduate himself. But here we are at Hillsdale, nearly one hundred fifty years later, still doing what we are supposed to do, and doing it well. What failure was there in this way of doing things? There was none.

Charity (*caritas*) in those days was likened unto a Christian vision of the city on the hill. Wealth was not an end in itself, but a means to enhance family, virtue and community. A speaker at the meeting I've referred to noted that charities then had the philosophy, "No relief given here!" That may sound very strange to us now, but it is in the highest spirit of charity: which is to help someone stand on his own and be what he can be; instead of becoming dependent on others' kindness. What the charities of the period did was found libraries, savings banks, day nurseries and other self-help institutions.

Religious belief diminished due to the Civil War, and after it, as scientism and Darwinism took hold and industry boomed. It seemed as if man could go it alone, without God, and liberty gave way to progress as our watchword. The whole idea of charity was overhauled to mean social insurance, after European examples, and it was only a short step from there to the idea of *entitlement*. What had been a gift from a well-meaning philanthropist became a *right* for the recipient. Our budding socialists even impugned the philanthropist's motives—how dare he feel good about doing good? That makes him better than the rest of us, when we are supposed to be equals. Shame on him! I trust you will see in this kind of thinking, as easily as I do, all the foundations of the modern welfare state, which taxes and shames the producers among us, and rewards the slackers and nonproducers as their *right*. They are told that they are entitled to other people's earnings and property, with no stigma attached. It breaks their human spirit.

In the same trends, the purposive charity gave way to the do-anything foundation. Managers of foundations were selected, not for the goodness of their heart, but for their science. This too was to become oh, so professional—instead of generous. Not surprisingly, the focused charitable impulse was thrown away in favor of the secular "social agenda," which works out to building the socialist utopia with capitalists' money.

And that is pretty much where we stand, both through the coercive measures of the government and through the enormous impact (though you do not hear about it) of the not-for-profit foundations. One trick the foundations all know about, and you probably do not, is leverage. They can spend *x* dollars to launch some socialized program that sounds high-minded. The next thing you know, we are paying twenty or fifty or two hundred times as much to support that same program with our taxes. The statists get a horse-laugh, all-too-literally at our expense. But they are, in doing so, running roughshod over the most basic human aspirations and justice, and I do not think the last laugh will be theirs.

Meanwhile, may I suggest that you investigate with great care any institution that claims it will do good with your gift or bequest? If you choose at random, or even by sweet-sounding presentations, the chances are, today, appallingly high that you will be financing your enemy. Look very closely.

Business

Obviously, there is no love lost on the left for American business. The left has been in the business-bashing trade ever since Marx made a mess of economics a century and a half ago. The shock is,

American business is almost swooning with love for the left and its agenda. You think the corporate world would know and fight its enemies. In truth, it subsidizes them, and very generously too. The left guards this secret carefully, quietly thanking its benefactors in private, then bashing them again in public—for instance in its portrayal of businessmen in movies and television shows, where they almost always turn out to be grasping, socially callous, ruthless criminals.

The facts are secret no more, thanks largely to Professor Marvin Olasky, author of *Patterns of Corporate Philanthropy*, and several colleagues who have dug into corporate records. Among their findings were that seventy percent of corporate donations with an identifiable political content go to liberal-left groups. "For example," writes Olasky, "six companies alone—AT&T, Citicorp, Dayton Hudson, Morgan Guaranty Trust, Standard Oil and Union Pacific—gave $132,000 in 1985 (the last year for which records are available) to Planned Parenthood, the nation's leading abortion provider. . . . " Similarly, corporate dollars are being used to promote homosexuality, racial quotas and radical feminism, along with abortion. Twenty-four of the one hundred largest corporations support the legal arm of the National Organization of Women. Would you like to know which? American Express, AT&T, Atlantic Richfield, Bell South, Burlington Northern, Chrysler, Coca-Cola, Dayton Hudson, Eastman Kodak, Federated Department Stores, General Motors, Goodyear, Johnson & Johnson, Manufacturers Hanover, Merrill Lynch, JC Penney, Philip Morris, RJ Reynolds, Standard Oil and Xerox. Twenty-four of the twenty-five largest corporations contributed more than a million and a half dollars to the Urban League and the NAACP, groups that lobby for racial quotas, more federal intervention in business, and more of the welfarist mire. Other recipients of corporate gifts include the Ms. Foundation, the Lesbian Resource Center, and Holding Our Own, a lesbian fundraising group. The most surprising donees are activist and environmentalist groups that use the money to sue business, in one case a group that exists solely to teach others *how* to sue corporations.

Clearly, some of this corporate generosity is an effort to appease or buy off its detractors. Just as clearly, this does not work at all. George Mason University Professor Walter Williams suspects that, in a handful of cases, the corporate donor may be using the radical group for competitive advantage. For instance, an oil company might be generous to an ecological group opposed to offshore drilling, and thereby thwart a competitor that could profit from the offshore oil.

But both of these factors would seem to be exceptions. In the main, support for the leftist agenda has crept into the corporate world just as it has invaded the philanthropies, as we have discussed above. Nobody is really in charge of donations in corporate offices. Thus again the moneys are turned over to professionals—"professional altruists," Irving Kristol calls them scornfully—who disburse it "scientifically." And again, it works out to supporting their own agenda and what is currently fashionable on the left.

Corporations do not have a collective soul. They cannot love humanity. Nor is it within their expertise to "do good" for humanity, even for PR reasons. The one way they really can help others is by making all the money they can. They do that by providing their goods and services better and cheaper than their competitors do. This benefits every one of their customers, who make their purchases freely precisely because they improve their own lives by doing so. This is barebones economics, going back to Adam Smith two centuries ago, and even earlier. In theory, the corporations should not be indulging in supposed philanthropy at all, but rather plowing those funds into improved productivity and into better pay, pensions and working conditions for their employees.

The most vexing part of this is that the business world is notoriously reluctant to defend itself, or advance its own self-interest, or even to finance groups that are willing and able to promote free enterprise and the market economy. It is as if business itself had drunk too deeply from the same old bottle of Marxist hooch. It acts as if it feels guilty about its success. Former Treasury Secretary William Simon points out, if business won't fight for its own legitimacy, others will naturally tend to think it corrupt.

It is ironic that the principal defenders of business and the market are academics and journalists, not businessmen. These defenders have long since learned that making the case for free markets is a great way to stay poor—because the corporate world, with a few exceptions, won't help. They defend the market because it is *right,* and will go on doing so. But they need a much stronger voice and wider audience. And in this, businessmen could help a great deal, if they were shown how and why.

Corporate giving is here to stay. But it is not carved in stone that such monies have to go to enemies of the market economy. There would seem much that individuals could do to wake up the corporations and direct their largesse to more responsible and productive ends. If you own so much as a single share of their stock, you are entitled to demand an accounting of where their dollars are going. Leftist activists know this, and often buy a share of stock just to make a row at annual meetings. If you own more shares, you can make a bigger row in reply. And you should. At least we oughtn't permit the liberal-left to turn corporations into their own private milk cows—by default.

* * *

In a sense, all these sad failings of our free institutions reflect our own failings. We have not fought hard enough to uphold our moral standards, nor discriminated in our charities and church work, nor defended in our daily business the freedom of markets that makes all our business possible. But we know the road back to sanity, and it begins with each of us doing our part. I see that happening more and more. The tide is turning.

Chapter XII
POWER TRIPS
America's Destructive Addiction to Politics

That government is no more than a choice among evils is acknowledged by the most intelligent among mankind, and has been a standing maxim for ages.

—Patrick Henry

The natural progress[ion] of things is for government to gain ground and for liberty to yield.

—Thomas Jefferson

There is, I think, only one revolutionary society in the contemporary world, and that is our society. It is so revolutionary that it's not clear that any of us can finally bear the daring thrust to the realization of the age-old values that our American revolution contains and celebrates.

Those values are the definitive values of Judeo-Christian civilization. They have inspired every authentically Judeo-Christian society in history. Those values declare, above all, the irreducible worth and uniqueness of every individual.

—Jeane Kirkpatrick

Albert Jay Nock marveled at the blind faith of those who think that the government is able to do just about anything and should. He observed that a week didn't pass without news of the failure of two government programs and demands for three new ones. Fifty years, and literally trillions of dollars worth of failures later, that faith is still with us, undimmed. The only difference is now we get seven disasters a week and demands for eleven new ones. I, too, marvel.

How is it that this thing called government can be thought of as almost godlike, even as nearly all experience is to the contrary? We all *know* all about the corruption and venality of politics and politicians. In recent times, many a mighty pol has fallen, including a president, a vice-president and a speaker of the House—the top three positions in government. One day we make the wobbly assumption that the person we elect to represent *us* is above all that and will really, truly go to Washington and cut taxes. The next thing we know is our taxes are up again and our representative is in jail for taking bribes. As M. Stanton Evans observes, when we elect our people to public office, they stop being our people. Power corrupts, and we all know that too. Why do we expect any other result?

We are addicted to shopping our problems, down to the last runny nose, to Washington even though we know the "solution," created in the wonderland of politics, will almost certainly pour money—our own money—down the rathole. The "solution" will also stick us with another law diminishing our freedom and a spanking new bureaucracy ready to do what bureaucracies do best: bungle. Bureaucracy has, after all, made it into the dictionary for its legendary blundering, bickering, and blockheadedness. It is awash in red tape and forms, in slowness and stupidity, in monumental waste and defiance of all sense. It cannot be anything else, for reasons I have explored elsewhere* and will not repeat here at any length. The principal reason is that coercive force is the only tool government has. Coercion is a hopelessly unsuitable tool for economic and social purposes. It is also endlessly abused, inherently destructive and an extremely dangerous interloper in the affairs of free people. Blind indeed is this faith that calls for even more political "solutions," when the miserable handiwork of previous attempts is before us.

America by the Throat: The Stranglehold of Federal Bureaucracy. Devin-Adair, Old Greenwich, Connecticut, 1983. Available in softcover, 1985 edition, from the Hillsdale College Press.

For those less blinded, the government answer to things is usually funny because it is so obviously wrongheaded. It would be much funnier if it weren't so wasteful of our freedom, our money and our patience! But I can still laugh about it, and so can the editors of *National Review,* who for many years have gleefully chronicled the strange ways of Uncle Sam (and all of his little children and friends in state, local and foreign governments). Over the years the pages of *NR* have become a sort of museum of governmental freaks and horrors. I am indebted to that excellent journal for many of the examples below, and believe me, this is just a tiny sampling. There are enough stories like these to fill a library. Later we will have to look at why things go so wildly amiss in government programs, which is depressing. So let's have a few laughs first at the supposedly godlike behavior of government. Any government. So far as I know, every bit of the following is true. Certainly I could not make it up.

Great Government Achievements You May Have Missed

The Agriculture Department launched a computerized dating service for goats. . . . The information officer [!] of the U.S. embassy in La Paz referred to Bolivians as "trolls . . . short and dark and strange, not like people, really, but humanlike to a certain extent. . . . " The Pentagon issued a fifteen-page recipe for a certain kind of cookie. . . . $75,000,000 in an anti-drug bill was earmarked for doing something about a telescope that fell over in West Virginia. . . . During its scandal years, HUD was under oversight by 84 congressional committees (is there anything they failed to overlook?). . . . A man who, without provocation, took a customer into a back room of a store, hit her repeatedly in the head with a hammer, then stabbed her repeatedly and left her for dead, soon became a top aide for the Speaker of the House (who knew about all this) earning $86,300 per year. . . . The State Department, in the course of issuing $15 million in erroneous travel advances, paid for the travels of Ludwig von Beethoven, perhaps unaware that he died in 1827. . . . The IRS issued its first rules that required the solving of quadratic equations, yielding more than one answer. . . . Sweden passed a bill of rights for farm animals. Animals can sue their owners for violations of rights. (What do they tell the judge? Moo? Oink?). . . . The Food and Drug Administration says it is fine to have up to 30 fly eggs in 3.5 ounces of tomato sauce, 700 insect fragments in a pound of flour, and 10 milligrams of rodent feces in a pound of cocoa beans. . . . A dog spayed in a local government program in Oregon had 12 puppies, all male. . . . The government uses 778,000,000 paper clips a year. It made 2,494,570 decisions in 1988 about how secret to classify secret classified documents. Its 1986 farm bill was 1,397 pages long . . . The legislature of Vermont passed a law to protect the monster in Lake Champlain, just in case anybody discovers one. . . . The mayor of Andalusia, Alabama, donned a turban and some rubber snakes and declared National Voodoo Week. This was hardly a year after the mayor of Florala, Alabama, sprinkled voodoo dust around city hall to drive out evil spirits (it didn't work). . . . The government has a cookbook for school lunches, with such delicacies as peanut butter and beef jerky sandwiches, tuna shortcake, and macaroni and cheese with 1,911 milligrams of sodium per serving. . . . "It is reported that the Congress of the United States sends out 12,000 pieces of mail for every piece it receives. Why so many people write back is beyond us," says *NR*. . . . Only 7,286 government officials were convicted of corruption in the decade 1977–86. . . . Three windmills—billed as a "multimegawatt wind farm"—built by the Energy Department for $60,000,000 did not quite work out as expected, and were later sold for scrap, for $28,000. . . . As of 1987, Italy was on its forty-seventh government since WWII. . . . The town of Horseshoe Bend, Idaho, adopted a 20-ton, 33-foot log as its mascot. . . . The biggest piece of federal legislation in 1986 was a tax reform bill. The biggest piece of legislation in 1987 was a bill correcting mistakes in the tax reform. . . . A lobby registered with Congress to protect and advance the rights of Witloof endive. . . . The world's largest scarecrow was erected in Vienna, Virginia, in 1986 by UNICEF.

But at Least the Government Is Maintaining Law and Order. . . .

The Supreme Court of New Hampshire had to address the question of how many belches are legal. . . . A man in Wyoming got 30 days in jail for fishing with a worm. . . . New York City arrested a man on charges of "eating the parks." . . . The defense minister of Liberia, his wife and seven others were charged with beheading a policeman and using his heart and other organs for black magic. . . . A man in Skegness, England, was fined $135 for fish neglect. . . . Federal agents seized a large batch of pink money, claiming that it was counterfeit (and that theirs was not). . . . After a three-month investigation and a heated debate, police in Indiana decided that a man who died of 32 hammer blows to the head had been murdered, and was not, as originally ruled, a suicide. . . . A New Jersey man was arrested for shooting his computer. . . . The justice system in Louisville, Kentucky, had a problem on its hands in trying, for drunk driving, a man who was in fact very drunk indeed, but who wasn't driving. His dog was at the wheel. . . . In Ohio, it is illegal to advertise beer if you are wearing a Santa Claus suit, including if you are a dog . . . . The government sued the Salvation Army for speaking English. . . . As of 1987, the longest-running trial in America had been going on two years. It concerned one teaspoon of spilled dioxin and may still be going on, for all I know. . . . Federal turtle police cracked down on 34 pet stores for selling federally impermissible turtles . . . . A court in West Germany ruled that the frogs in Mr. Lars Wendt's pond are free to croak in mating season. . . . The city fathers of Cedar Rapids started ticketing trains for blowing their whistles at crossings, which they are required by law to do. . . . Muttering that "being Chief of State is an extremely thankless job," former Emperor Bokassa I of the Central African Republic went on trial for homicide, infanticide, embezzlement, treason, torture, theft and cannibalism.

Some Ways of Funding these Worthy Activities that You Also May Have Missed

The politicians of Fort Collins, Colorado, made a game effort to tax Girl Scout cookies, but were defeated by public ridicule. . . . A small businessman in Arkansas, after filling out 200 forms for the IRS, was told he was subject to a $50 fine for using the wrong typewriter—for each and every form. That's $10,000 in fines and $150 for a new typewriter. . . .

Guess who applied for a $56 million federal business development grant, available to communities suffering "physical and economic distress"? Beverly Hills. . . . China says taxes are a "glorious responsibility." . . . The state of Indiana tried to impose inheritance taxes on pets. . . . In case you plan to fish with your spawn sack containing salmon roe or imitation roe made out of dyed marshmallows scented with anise or crayfish oils, please remember to pay your 10 percent excise tax to the federal government, which has its own ways of fishing. . . . U.S. customs agents tossed 29,000 bottles of rum into a dumpster and smashed it all, $100,000 worth, not because it was illegal or smuggled into the country, but because the importer was broke and couldn't afford the tariffs and taxes. . . . The city of New Orleans, presumably desperate for revenue, sent out a crew of workers and meter maids. The workers reversed one-way-street signs, and the meter maids then ticketed all the cars parked in the "wrong" direction.

We conclude with a tale that combines all the features of bureaucracy we have looked at into one monumental stupidity. The teller of this tale is Dave Barry, a very funny man:

"Recently I read this news item stating that the U.S. Senate Finance Committee had printed up 4,500 copies of a 452-page document with every single word crossed out. The Senate Finance Committee did this on purpose. It wasn't the kind of situation where they got the document back from the printer and said, 'Hey! Every single word in this document is crossed out! We are going to fire the zitbrain responsible for this!' A 452-page document with all the words crossed out was exactly what the Senate Finance Committee wanted.

"This news item intrigued me. I said to myself, there must be a logical explanation for this. So I called Washington, D.C., and over the course of an afternoon I spoke to, I don't know, maybe 15 or 20 people, and sure enough it turned out there was an extremely logical explanation: The Senate Finance Committee was following The Rules.

"Okay. Everybody understand the point here? The point is: You have to follow The Rules. Without rules, you would have ANARCHY.

"And that is exactly why the Senate Finance Committee had to print up 4,500 copies of a 452-page document with every single word crossed out. What this document was, originally, was the tax reform bill passed by the House of Representatives. It seems the Senate Finance Committee didn't like it, so they wrote a whole new bill, with all different words. Their new bill is 1,489 pages long. Also, they wrote another 1,124 pages to explain how it works. (Sounds like our new reformed tax system is going to be mighty simple, all right! I can't wait!)

"Okay. So the Finance Committee had 2,613 pages worth of tax reform to print up, but that was not all. They also printed up the entire House bill, the one they rejected, with all the words crossed out to show where they disagreed with it. According to the 15 or 20 people I talked to on the phone, the committee had to do this. I asked them if maybe it wouldn't have been more economical, and just as informative, if the Finance Committee had simply stuck a little note on the front of their bill, saying something like: 'We thought the whole House Bill was pig doots, and we chucked it out,' but the 15 or 20 people assured me that, no, this was not possible under The Rules.

"By the way: This document is for sale. This is the truth. You can actually buy a document that your government has used your tax money to print up with all the words crossed out. It's called HR 3838 As Reported in the Senate, Part I. The Government Printing Office is selling it for—I swear—$17. So far they have sold 1,800 copies, and **I don't even want to know** who is buying them. I am sure that whoever they are, they're going to claim every single cent they spent on these documents as a tax deduction, but I don't care. I'm through asking questions."

See what I mean? So much for omnipotence and goodness of the institution some think can solve all our problems. Think what would happen to the price of bread if bakers and truckers and grocers had to follow rules like these! Sooner or later we are going to have to learn to get things done by ourselves, if the government doesn't land us in the poorhouse (or the madhouse) first.

The Futility of Government Intervention

The earliest written records we have found are wage-price controls, imposed by a benevolent monarch in the utterly futile attempt to make the will, and arms, of a ruler succeed, where only the wishes of free people, expressed in the market, can. After eight thousand years of trying to dictate economics by state coercion, and failing miserably every time, you'd think we would learn something.

The examples we have seen, and an unlimited number of others like them, are not what goes on in *normal* life. Things go so well in our everyday lives that veritable miracles occur and we never notice. You need coffee, toilet paper, a coat, a bottle of unchlorinated water, new tires, a book? You simply go to the appropriate store and buy them, if the price is right. The goods are there for you. If it turns out that you can't find just the right item, there are alternatives that you can buy, or not, at your wish. The shelves are full. This is natural for us and we take it for granted—but we shouldn't. In the long history of mankind, this state of affairs is so rare as to be almost unbelievable.

Consider. When we buy, say, a can of pork and beans, we get (for a sum measured in pennies, not dollars) the product of many industries, all working cooperatively to put what we need before us, when we want it, at a price we can afford—without any government action involved at all. The can itself may have come out of the iron mines of the Mesabi, mined, carted, smelted, refined and shaped by processes too complex for any one person to understand, then coated in tin mined in Burma and sent across the seas, thanks to many more industries. All of the ingredients that go into the can: the beans, the pork, the tomato sauce, the spices, are again products of the whole world acting in concert; all to put that can of pork and beans on the grocer's shelf when you want it.

About this two things should be said. First, this is the whole essence of social cooperation. Second, your decision to buy or not to buy that can of beans drives vast industries. It happens because and only because you have the freedom of choice. In this I include everything that goes into freedom of choice, not least real rights of life, liberty and property, accepted by all and protected by tradition, custom and law; and underlying these, the whole moral basis of Western civilization, that sees us as children of God and not as beasts to be pushed about for the convenience of the state. Either we are unique, self-controlling individuals, each of whose lives has transcendent purpose, or we will wear rags, will not have enough to eat, and will sleep in hovels on the naked earth—as has been the fate of most of mankind for most of recorded history. Except as we are free, with all that this implies, our economic miracles will vanish, and we can take our place in food lines or riot over prices like so much of the world does even now. Free markets are what employ us, feed us and clothe us, and do so with a luxury that would have been the envy of the mightiest rulers of old. Nothing else can.

It is when we revert to the thinking and methods of kings and Caesars and pharaohs that we get into big-time trouble. The federal government has no better and no different tools than the pharaoh, except perhaps more sophistication at the old stand, and the results are no better today than they were 6,000 years ago in Egypt. As Mises so forcefully reminded us, "There are [only] two methods for the conduct of affairs within the frame of human society. . . . One is bureaucratic management, the other is profit management." It was no advantage, he said, to dispose of profit (incorrectly conceived by Marxism as an ill-gotten gain), because without it, bureaucratic managers are deprived of any feedback from markets and real prices, and are totally blind as to whether what they do is worthwhile or not. This is the fatal failing of all central (that is, governmental) planning. So persuasively did Mises make this essential point seventy years ago that the chief ideologist of the Soviet revolution, Trotsky, embraced it with hosannahs. But the Soviet Union did not, and thus suffered three generations of blindness—the substitution of a handful of state planners for the wishes and plans of all the people, by naked force. This produces nothing. It merely impedes what real production there is.

There are three qualities common to all government intrusion into private life. First, all bureaucracy is empowered by, and is the executor of, coercive government controls. Every attempt at bureaucratic management is an extension of coercive government controls into a previously free and private area of life. It is an effort, in other words, to dictate by force what had been done person to person, through persuasion and cooperation, according to our private moral values and rational economic calculation.

A word or two about what I mean by "coercion." It refers to the use, or threatened use, of force, to compel people to behave in a certain way. All laws and regulations are coercive in nature. Coercion is the one central feature of government sovereignty. Governments have, and are supposed to have, a monopoly on the use of force. All government undertakings are based on the use of compulsion. All private coercion—that is, where one person uses force to make another surrender property or do his bidding—is criminal. This is as it should be. Yet compulsion, governmental as well as private, is the most dangerous of instruments, and is all too easily extended into areas where it does not belong. We would never try to run a farm or factory on the same coercive principles that are needed to run a police station. Yet this is precisely what we attempt to do when we seek, or accede to, government controls over business, labor, wages, prices, schools, churches and other plainly private areas of life. The controls are then administered by a bureau that is coercive in nature, and we experience all the ills that result from using compulsion where it does not belong. And more often than not, we end up wondering what went wrong. The answer is that we should not have put cops in charge of our farms and factories.

The second quality of government intrusion flows from the axiom that sovereigns never surrender their power voluntarily. Said Patrick Henry, "Human nature will never part from power. Look for an example of a voluntary relinquishment of power, from one end of the globe to another—you will find none. . . . Can you say that you will be safe when you give such unlimited powers without any real responsibility? Will not the members of Congress have the same passions which other rulers have had?" (Henry was objecting to the proposed Constitution. His and similar objections from others had such weight as to require adding the Bill of Rights before the Constitution could be ratified.) This axiom has a direct and immediate effect on the way Congress creates a new bureau. On the one hand, it must delegate power to the bureau. On the other hand, it must retain its sovereignty over the bureau; obviously it cannot be allowed to do what it pleases or help itself to funds from the Treasury. The one and only answer is for Congress to rule the bureau with the Rulebook. *The supreme duty of every government agency is to follow The Rules*. One may argue that the *only* duty of a bureau is to follow The Rules. Which is what Mr. Barry so amusingly discovered. The implications of this are far-reaching. Here, for instance, we find out why government actions are so notoriously rigid and unresponsive. What else can they be, if their duty is to the Rulebook? It cannot serve the particular needs of those it is pleased to call its "clients." Rather, the clients' needs must be pushed, pulled, manipulated or abandoned according to how they fit, or do not fit, the Rulebook. The By-The-Rules approach also explains why the best agency head can do little better than the worst. Neither has the discretion to make sweeping changes. What discretion they have covers only internal matters or minor rules; they cannot alter their mission. Many other annoyances and outrages of bureaucratic management are similarly traceable directly to the Rulebook. But there is no other way a government agency can function.

Profit management is based on the realities of prices, wages, productivity and the balance sheet. It must respond to reality, or face bankruptcy. It could do nothing right if forced to operate by a rulebook instead of being flexible enough to act with rational calculation. There are few places in life suited for inflexible Rules. We do things by give and take, compromise, what's right for a given situation, what's right for one person but not necessarily for another. We bend and adapt all the time. The Rules don't bend and don't work.

There is more. Rules corrupt. Every rule creates economic

privilege for some and an unjust disadvantage for others. This is corrupt in itself, and it creates endless temptations for further corruption, by those who seek privilege, and by those in the bureaucracy for whom it represents more power. A better breeding ground for injustice and social resentments can hardly be devised. Worse, it offers a tailor-made excuse to all who have been cheated to join in the corruption. After all, they can say with some justice. "I've been cheated and I want to get even," or "Everybody else is getting theirs, so why shouldn't I get mine?" As has been observed many times, once government starts handing out favors to some, it is obliged to give favors to everyone—at everyone else's expense. Wrote Henry George, "To introduce a tariff bill into congress or parliament is like throwing a banana into a cage of monkeys. No sooner is it proposed to protect one industry than all the industries that are capable of protection begin to screech and scramble for it." He added: "All experience shows that the policy of [state] encouragement, once begun, leads to a scramble in which it is the strong, not the weak; the unscrupulous, not the deserving, that succeed. What are really infant industries have no more chance in the struggle for governmental encouragement than infant pigs have with full grown swine about a meal tub."

The third distinguishing characteristic of bureaucratic management is that it is wholly political in nature and operates in a nonmarket, not-for-profit setting. The importance of this lies less in what a governmental agency is than in what it lacks, so let me put it this way: All bureaucracy functions outside the marketplace; no market-determined need exists for its services, and there is no objective relationship between its revenues and its expenditures.

Government bodies, in a word, cannot calculate the value of what they do. They cannot even use double-entry bookkeeping, the standard tool of business. It seems hard to believe, but no bureau, agency or congressional committee ever truly *knows* that what it is doing is worth anything. It is equally in the dark if its actions are fruitful or destructive. It just doesn't know, and cannot know. There is no economic feedback to learn from, no prices, no balance sheet. Its efforts cannot be measured by private business tools. It can employ only opinion to assess its own efforts, and political opinion at that. It will hear mainly from lobbyists and interest groups with political axes to grind, not from the people. Washington, D.C.—a city of northern charm and southern efficiency, as someone put it—is famous (or infamous) for its inside-the-beltway mentality. It lives in a world of intrigue and politics, and is deaf to the rest of the country. But what else can it do? It has no economic tools to assess its own efforts, so must rely on politics for everything. Small wonder the place seems crazy to everyone else!

You and I, and no one else, know what's best for us, in what we produce and consume, and that is what makes markets. A state mechanism has no objective means of ascertaining reality. The political solution here, today, or anywhere, anytime, is equally blind. It cannot assess results, as a business manager can read a profit and loss statement, so it must resort to *The Rules,* and to an equally political assessment of the results of applying The Rules. But The Rules say nothing about real performance. They just tell us to arrest people for eating parks or to print 452-page documents with every single word crossed out—at your expense. The whole system works out to precisely what Mises said, that either you accept the market information in profit management, or you fly in the dark and crash—as every socialist venture has crashed. "[Competitive markets are] the only means so far discovered of enabling individuals to coordinate their economic activities without coercion," says Nobel Laureate economist Milton Friedman.

Let me put things even more simply in today's vernacular: Either you make it or you take it. There are no other choices. If you take it, you are either in the robbery business or in government. Washington has nothing to give that it does not first take. When you ask the politicians for something, and if they oblige, you are taking it away from somebody else. You are taking bread off their table. You are stealing their work. Now it may very well be that when you do this you are full of good intentions, and armed with any number of rationalizations about how the person you are stealing for has been disadvantaged by the system, is in need, and so on. But do you give any thought to the fact that the people you are taking from are in need too, are being disadvantaged by what you do, and are entitled to keep what they earned? The market system, which is people freely working together, creates wealth. The political system creates poverty and injustice. We must break our long addiction to it, or it will break us. Just say no.

Chapter XIII

A BRIGHTER ROAD AHEAD—
AT LAST

"The best thing is that for the first time we don't have to whisper. I can say what I think, I can shout it." And she does: "Communism stinks!"
— Romanian housewife, quoted shortly after the fall of the Romanian communist government

It is faith, creativity, altruism, generosity, the impulse of giving without any assured return, and the willingness to invest despite an always bleak and perilous future that accounts for human triumph and the success of capitalism.

— George Gilder

In a world of voluntary social cooperation whether one man's gain is another man's *gain*, it is obvious that great scope is provided for the development of social sympathy and human friendships. It is the peaceful, cooperative society that creates favorable conditions for feelings of friendship among men.

— Charles Murray

I am an example of the small person who can do great things. I am proof of the adage that faith can move mountains.

— Lech Walesa

We are living in a springtime of liberty, mind and spirit. When I started writing this book a year and a half ago, no one could have imagined that country after country in Eastern Europe would throw off its communist yoke. Even more surprising, these extraordinary events occurred almost without bloodshed, except in Stalinist Romania. But in the Christmas season we all watched a very special celebration in Berlin, and we knew the impossible dream had come true. East and West Berliners, reunited after twenty-eight years, hugged and laughed and poured champagne and wept and defiantly danced on that monument to barbarity that had divided them, the Berlin Wall. Uncounted millions around the world wept and laughed with them, and church bells rang. Here, for all the world to see, was the symbolic reunion of long-divided Europe and of the world, in freedom and in a rebirth of civilization.

Here, too, all saw that communism was no longer a potent idea contending for the minds and hearts of men. It was just one more instrument of power, naked power of men over men, such as we have seen countless times before in history, and understand. Its last pretensions as a moral idea collapsed as its borders were broken. The crimes it had so long concealed were laid bare; it lay in the destruction and reek of its own works, economically exhausted and spiritually destitute. To the inquiring souls among the younger generation, communism must seem like some evil, forgotten sect whose incantations and chants were like witch doctors shaking bones. (Whatever did they *mean* by dialectical materialism or the surplus labor theory of value?) Those of us who have been through more of the struggle may find these events more like wakening in surprise and immense relief as a nightmare ends. I do not believe the nightmare will ever come back. Communism has nothing left with which to move men.

I had not dreamt of anything like this even while writing, in Chapter VIII, that socialism was dead. I meant that the doctrine was no longer intellectually tenable on any terms. But I was no more a prophet about how soon this would be proven in Eastern Europe than anyone else. I had added my puzzlement that there was no corresponding celebration of capitalism, and here too I was off the mark—I'm tickled to say. There was—and is—in Prague and Warsaw and Budapest, and even in Moscow. Obviously, we in the West take our market economy too much for granted. It has been more admired, and at times better understood, where it was absent and where the brunt of a coercive system was felt everyday. In fact, there was a poll taken among ordinary citizens in Moscow with this question: "Which system do you think is superior to the other, socialism or capitalism?" Response: capitalism 51 percent, socialism 32 percent. I'm glad they didn't poll Harvard.

My favorite story about this is of the huge Institute of Marxism-Leninism in Prague, Czechoslovakia, that was disbanded as soon as the communist rulers were tossed out. That is, all except for the Department of Bourgeois Economics which had been set up to study our ideas in order to use them against us. Unfortunately for the plan, the people in that department were converted by reading Hayek, Mises, Friedman, et al. They joked afterward that the only remaining Marxist true believers are in American universities. Yes, we've heard it, but do *we* have free-market departments on most college campuses? The joke is doubly on us! Said their new finance minister, "The world is run by human action, not by human design"—a plain reference to Mises' masterwork, *Human Action*. One of Hillsdale College's proudest possessions is the personal library of Ludwig von Mises, who left the entire annotated collection of his beloved books to Hillsdale College, which he described as " . . . that educational institution which most strongly represents the free market ideas to which I have given my life."

Events still swirl as I write, too swiftly for me or anyone to foresee how they will end. It is not going to be easy for Eastern Europeans to rebuild their decimated economies, or to relearn the ways of entrepreneurial capitalism after four decades of suppression. They will have to reinstitute property rights, and I'm not sure how this can be done in such states. But they have three things going for them that give me great hope. First, they have their churches back—churches that were, in fact, highly instrumental in the downfall of communist rule, by their teaching and moral leadership. Churches had a leading role in every one of the countries involved, and have the same leadership in some that still seek their freedom. Second, they know at least the theory of free markets—I think they could teach us a thing or two—and have intense experience in how not to do it, so need not waste their energies on false solutions. Third, in large measure, they have their freedom back. Freedom is what makes everything work. We don't know quite how, because we can't predict what free men and women will do; but we can be confident that they will find ways to make things work.

Something I've noticed that hasn't been mentioned anywhere is how incredibly direct and blunt the new leaders in Eastern Europe are. They talk as if they had long been truth-starved, as indeed they were, and use none of the evasions or nuances of politicians. And they tell us incredible things. All this time, forty years or more, they say, they were *cheated*. Communism was a *hoax*. It wasted their hard labor. It left them with nothing. Worse, it made war on their spirit and left behind "a decayed moral environment," in the words of Vaclav Havel, president of Czechoslovakia. Back in 1984, an East German girl, wise beyond her years, sadly told a visitor from the West: "It doesn't make any difference what we become when we grow up. We will still always be treated like children." She was saying, like Havel, that the very fulfillment of life through adult responsibility and moral choice was impossible under communist suppression. Lech Walesa, only the second foreigner in our history to address a joint session of Congress (the first was Lafayette), made just such points in his historic speech.

Others—God bless the human spirit that can laugh after all it went through—said the same thing with jokes. Here is the wry assessment of an East German: The six miracles of socialism:

— There is no unemployment, but no one works.
— No one works, but everyone gets paid.
— Everyone gets paid, but there's nothing to buy with the money.
— No one can buy anything, but everyone owns everything.
— Everyone owns everything, but no one is satisfied.
— No one is satisfied, but 99 percent of the people vote for the system.

The Shameless Among Us

For all these years, the left in this country has claimed that socialism is morally superior to our market system. They criticized every aspect of America, all the while chanting their chants and rattling their bones. They compared our "failures," real or more often imagined, with their utopian pipe dreams.

Through *glasnost* and the testimony of Eastern Europeans, we know that the truth was exactly the opposite of the socialists' promise *in every case*. In the name of "equality" and "economic justice," the party bosses gave themselves a cut of the wealth one hundred to one thousand times greater than the masses. This differential in wealth is vastly greater than under capitalism. They created a ruling class, the *nomenklatura,* more autocratic and exploitive than the tsars. In a system much like apartheid, except far more virulent, they reserved for themselves all the top jobs, the best education, the best medical care and up to 100 percent of the quality goods, sold in special stores which only they could patronize. So shamelessly did and do they bleed workers that 86.5 percent of the Soviet population, by a Soviet report, are dirt poor. Many have never had running water or electricity. Only 11.2 percent of the population are well enough off to be called middle class. (In the West, the figure is usually 50 percent to 70 percent.) That leaves just 2.3 percent with virtually all the power and privilege; and among these there is a "super-elite" of about 400,000 people who alone have access to such luxuries as the system is able to import. The promises were all frauds. "Power to the people" turns out to be totalitarian power in the hands of a tiny, highly privileged, ruling class. "Economic justice" turns out to be rank exploitation. The "worker's paradise" is in truth a grimy, alcohol-soaked, unbelievably polluted hell.

Now a lot of us never believed a word of this. To those of us who kept the faith, the socialist "vision" always did look like hell on earth, not utopia. It rebelled against God, denied the infinite worth of human life, and trampled liberty, diversity and excellence in the name of a joyless "equality." What place is there in such a scheme for one life on the human scale, one life well lived?

But many did believe and apparently still do. Their litany goes on undiminished in the media, in pulpits, in academe. They still call for more doses of the same old poisons: more controls, more taxes, more government. They still war on liberty and God. They are still the slavering servants of Pharaoh. But sooner or later the overwhelming weight of facts must overcome dreams and fantasies. We have long since passed the point where this should have happened.

To me, the loudest sound in these momentous events is the silence of those culpable of aiding and abetting the whole evil scheme. For years, we have heard them excuse or deny or resist every report of the brutality and misery in the communist system. Such monstrous acts as genocide, slave labor camps, biological warfare against helpless civilians, and booby-trapping toys to blow the limbs off Afghani children: even these were pooh-poohed or defended by people among us. By rights, these apologists of evil should be on their knees, begging the forgiveness of God and man. They were culpable in unforgivable crimes. But they are unrepentant and say nothing. The silence is deafening.

Freedom's Surprising Advance

I made a little calculation a while ago that I think you'll find interesting. About 200 years ago an English newspaper wrote, "Slaves are three and twenty times more numerous than men enjoying, in any tolerable degree, the rights of human nature." I estimate now that the ratio has fallen in the last two centuries from 23-to-1 to about 3-to-1. So, we've got a long way to go, but there's progress.

—Milton Friedman

Most conspicuously, we are seeing a decline in the power of governments, and also other institutions that mediate between people. This is the meaning of Tiananmen Square and Wenceslas Square. In a sense, William Shockley [inventor of transistors] produced Mikhail Gorbachev. A censor can tell what books are being brought through customs, but he'll never be able to keep track of the computer disks. And we're finding that totalitarian states cannot survive the information revolution. Back in the 1950s, wags talked of conquering Russia by bombarding it with Sears & Roebuck catalogues; the policy, unwittingly followed, has been an astounding success.

—Robert Bartley, Editor, the *Wall Street Journal*,
in a report on the 1980s.

The decade of the 1980s was bad news for Big Brother. The cause of freedom blossomed not only in Eastern Europe but around the world. According to a Freedom House Survey, 1989 was the pivotal year for freedom in the postwar period. It estimates that just over two billion people now live in freedom, 38.87 percent of the world population. "It's the freest the world has ever been," says the director. Another 1.14 billion (21.85 percent) live in partial freedom, that is, in formal democracies, but those with such problems as violence or abuse of the role of law. Unfortunately, another two billion (39.28 percent) are still denied liberty.

However, that is not the whole story. This survey could not keep up with fast-breaking events (nor can I). It still had listed among not-free nations Hungary, Czechoslovakia, Romania, East Germany, Bulgaria, and Panama. With unrest rumbling through the Soviet bloc and even within the U.S.S.R., it seems certain that more nations will soon gain independence.

As these nations adopt democracy and market systems, we can dramatically update Freedom House's estimate. Today, for the first time in history, a greater number of the world's people are free than are not. Another one in three enjoy some freedoms. Also for the first time, free countries outnumber the unfree.

That is a far cry from the state of things ten years ago. Over the period, at least thirty-six countries have ended dictatorship or military rule, as opposed to merely ten (mostly small) ones that slid back into oppression. I'll bet things will be rosier still when I write my A.D. 2000 book! But we have more to do here than celebrate. We have to look beneath the surface of these great events of the 1980s so that we can plan for the road ahead.

I believe that the age-old war between the individual and the Old World-type state has changed, fundamentally, in favor of the individual. I further believe that this is largely due to the vision of free and clear-eyed men who have created an awesome new arsenal against unwarranted state intervention. In doing so, they have enhanced the liberty of all.

Let's give some credit to our American vision of limited, constitutional self-government, too, for without it, we would not have had the freedom to create this amazing new world. With it, free men have disarmed the state's main weapons for subjugation. The guarded border has turned into a sieve. Unlimited taxation has been turned into a competition, among governments, to see who offers the lowest marginal rates. Bureaucratic regulations, protectionist policies, exchange controls (state efforts to prevent the movement of money), and similar state tools to keep a tax monopoly over their "subjects" are similarly being broken. In our new circumstances, governments must compete to offer the freest trade and soundest currency: if they want to retain the production of the free. If they do not, they will be left in the dust by those that offer better terms to enterprise.

Free men know what tyrants never learn, that the ultimate economic resource is the mind and energy of a free person. From a free mind only comes the direction of all productivity and the innovation that is tomorrow's prosperity. It is said that we live in an information economy now. This is true enough, but it is not the whole picture. Add to it an unprecedented mobility for the movement of economic resources—assets as well as data—and unheard of versatility in doing so. Thought and money can and do travel almost anywhere in a split second, too nimbly and fast for the plodding state to catch. It is this mobility that gives individuals the upper hand at last. There is no turning back.

My favorite part of this story is what resources free men have used to achieve it. For two centuries we have been haunted by an essay by Thomas Malthus calculating that we would have too many people with too few resources. His reasoning was terribly flawed, and the world has grown immeasurably in population and wealth since. But there are plenty who love to believe the worst, and they keep telling us we are running out of resources, and will all end up standing on each other's shoulders if we don't starve first. A prominent doomsayer of the 1970s predicted massive starvation in the 1980s. Oops! It's fun to see a doomsayer fall on his nose, but such talk is not funny at all. What we get out of it is government controls and resource rationing, and worse, a view that people are a bad thing, using up dwindling resources and "overpopulating," which leads to more government controls like stiff immigration laws. Against that tired, backward mindset, the real pioneers were even then creating a new world of silicon and iron oxide. Sand and rust! These are the main components for creating, recording and transmitting information around the world instantly. Back in the 1960s some daring soul predicted that there would be 220,000 computers by the year 2000. In fact, by 1990, there were more than 45 million in use, all of them able to link up with each other or with financial markets and other information networks, over the phone.

From sand and rust we get audio and video recorders and players (including, alas, boom boxes), the tapes and disks that computers use to record, and most important of all, the computers themselves. And, I gather, a lot of other devices I am even less qualified to talk about—but I can enjoy the parade, can't I? We can create information with sand and rust. We can beam it around the world on old-fashioned wires or new-fangled optical cable (sand) or bounce it off communications satellites. This is a free man's tool with a vengeance, and only free men may use it well, for it is a real and unstoppable channel for facts, truth and even faith.

Truth and faith are what repressive regimes must suppress, and they can do it no more. Not too long ago it was an easy thing for them, by inspections at the borders and by jamming radio. Now it is impossible. VCRs, copiers, FAX machines and computers have all become tools of *samizdat,* self-publishing, that shred the state monopoly on what people may know. A simple, cheap computer printer will provide unlimited copies. A diskette costing less than a dollar and weighing less than an ounce can hold as many words as a book. Already available or in the works are dozens of other devices that will create and disseminate far more information with far less chance of state interference. The day that a dictator could control what his "subjects" could hear, see and learn, and therefore what they think, is over. This was dramatically shown in Eastern Europe, where everyone knew what was going on in the other countries. Demonstrations for freedom in one country followed those in another almost overnight.

The same tools are used to allocate capital for its most productive uses in 24-hour markets around the globe. We can't afford to think about economic competition between nations any more, Mr. Bartley tells us. Companies increasingly operate in world markets and tap into international pools of capital and labor. It makes no difference where the company headquarters is located. Neither, interestingly, does it matter what race or color or creed runs the company. There is no room in the market for politics or bigotry or intolerance, for these just waste money and lose out to more efficient competitors. The old dream of "one world" is coming true, not under one great World State, but in world markets joined for cooperative and productive effort. The market world is directed by free men acting on their own good judgment, and their judgment is bringing the politicians of the world to account.

The most striking thing about this vast and growing "one world" market is that it severely limits the reach of the state. Governments control a given place, but the place you are matters little for doing business today. You can always set up shop in another place, and you can do it in hours, wiring your capital and records ahead or carrying all your files with you on computer disks. In other words, if one place doesn't treat you well, you can easily move to another, taking your capital and productivity with you. Too bad for the place that didn't treat you right: It just lost your economic contribution and your taxes.

I am simplifying, of course, but the factors I describe are real, and widespread, and growing fast. They are the reason that governments must increasingly compete for business favor with lower tax rates and a better economic climate. Says Mr. Bartley, "The global information network renders almost instant verdicts on changes in government policy. In the end, the world is ruled not by politicians but by markets." Tax rates have in fact been tumbling all over the world since the United States cut its top marginal rates early in the Reagan administration. Other overgrown governments—eventually even Sweden—were forced to copy us. The Reagan revolutionaries, including some very canny free market economists, deserve a lot more credit for this than they have received. The same competition is at work in chipping off years of bureaucratic barnacles. It enforces deregulation and privatization. It is a powerful impetus toward securing the rights of property and liberty. It has tidal force, I believe, in the worldwide movement to democracy and consequent collapse of communism. These trends can only grow stronger, as the mobility of the market grows and the grip of government weakens.

A great deal more is involved here than commerce. There is new freedom percolating in science, medicine and invention, and excitement is in the air. I know nothing about magnetic resonance imaging or chaos theory or a dozen other marvels, but I think we can learn something from them. What they tell me, at least, is that thinking that had become sterile or ingrown or dead-ended from long effort in one direction, has broken free in another direction and become creative again. The old direction we know too well: secularism and materialism. Today, we are seeing a sea-change, an outburst of fertile thought and work—work, moreover, at odds with a materialist view of life. We know that ideas have consequences. From the consequences we see today, we know that secularism has failed at some deep level. Science, freed of its grip, is in full bloom, pouring its achievements into our homes, our pharmacies, our fields, our lives. Communism, the purest political expression of secularism, is dying. Here, too, a nightmare ends, and the future is restored to the free, if we will but accept our responsibility.

By no means are we out of the woods, and we know that some battles are never won. But the legacies of the 1980s decade are almost all in one direction, and inspiring. Do you remember the demonstrators chanting "peace and freedom" in the tormented sixties? We got neither. But both peace and freedom broke out in the eighties, precisely because we stopped listening to the radicals and began to rely on our own hearts and sense again. America became normal and whole again, in the eyes of most.

There is an important idea underlying both the movement to democracy and the growth of the international marketplace: That the collective judgment of free people is wiser and fairer than judgments imposed by an entrenched political minority. Granted, democracy has its weaknesses, and free elections are no guarantor of freedom; but it is better than guaranteed unfreedom under a dictatorship. There are no equivalent weaknesses in collective judgment expressed in the market. Everybody (including children) can and does "vote," and every dollar counts. What each of us says by buying or not buying, investing or not investing, is: this is what is right for me, as an individual, according to my values. The collective judgment thus takes into account the most pressing needs of all, as each of us sees them (and each of us knows best what they are; certainly we know much better than any faraway bureaucrat). This judgment is *necessary* to direct all production so that it most efficiently and fairly provides what we want. It cannot be done by planners.

I stress this idea that the collective judgment is fairer, because it reflects a deeper view of ourselves that is the very basis of civilization. It reflects, indeed, the view of the Declaration of Independence, that all men are created equal and are endowed by God with the rights of life, liberty and the pursuit of happiness. Without these rights there can be no market, and without a market we cannot get enough to eat, much less reclaim our natural rights.

The surprising story of the 1980s, one new in history, is that the growing power of the world marketplace is bringing these facts home everywhere. Its power exposed the spiritual weakness of communism and helped tear down the Iron Curtain. Its power is moral and deserves all the moral support we can give it. Its message to every ruler on earth is: We are not things to be used by you, but free people with inalienable rights. In the market it does not matter how we came into the world but what we make of ourselves. In the market we join in cooperative effort for the good of all. If you interfere, you harm all people. If you oppress us, you will lose all that we have to offer and become poor. Throw away your chains and your barbed wire; they are useless now. Renounce rule and join us as the world moves on to peace, prosperity and freedom.

Good News Down Home

> How small, of all that human hearts endure,
> That part which laws or kings can cure!
> Still to ourselves in every place consigned,
> Our own felicity we make or find.
> —Samuel Johnson

We don't have to look to Eastern Europe or world markets for good news. It's right in our backyard. This is a fabulous time for people who are fed up with bureaucracy, or worse, government "solutions" that foul our world. The great old American tradition of getting things done on our own is back, and with it, the old "can do," thumbs-up spirit. What could be more welcome? More and more, "just plain folks" are taking charge and working minor miracles with few if any resources beyond their own courage and imagination.

It is really a blessing *not* to have handfuls of government money to throw at problems, and especially, not to have all the rules and red tape. When you and I, as private citizens, take a leadership role, we look at the problems as we face them in reality. We know other people involved in the process. We can gauge the effects of what we do in a very personal way. We can plan realistically with the resources we command, instead of forever clamoring for more taxes. We can feel, far better than any distant politician, what our own community needs and how it will respond. Best of all, there is the fulfillment for all of us, as individuals, that can come only by meeting our responsibilities and sharing our human sympathies. The most human of all stories during the collapse of communism in Eastern Europe was never told, at least that I heard. I mean the intense hunger of people to be responsible moral agents. This had been suppressed for forty long years or more by totalitarian governments which monopolized doing good. (Never mind that they made a complete botch of it.) It would not have occurred to Marx or Lenin or their followers that we *need* to take care of ourselves and our own; that we need the fulfillment of what we can make of ourselves, and not the stifling atmosphere state agencies give us. We cannot do good deeds by proxy. Doing good by proxy, with other people's money, is liberalism's stock in trade and the shallowest of illusions. The same illusion was shattered in Eastern Europe; may it be shattered here soon. We have to be ourselves, and when we are, we do wonders.

I'd like to share a few of these stories with you, a few out of the great number I have collected. There are stories like these in every area of human endeavor. I could cite examples from science or business or the fine arts and they are no less noble. As George Gilder has observed, " . . . all human pioneers, from poets and composers in their many epiphanies to scientists on the mystical frontiers where life begins, are essentially engaged in forms of devotion." But we don't have to be pioneers or poets. Loving our neighbors, and taking charge when called on to help them in need, is just as much a form of devotion. This we all can do. Unsung Americans do it every day. Most of their stories are never told, but enough are that we can delight in the joys of just being neighborly. I myself am amazed at the ingenuity and diversity of successes they achieve. See if you don't agree.

Let's start with a gentleman who spoke to us at Hillsdale not long ago: Steve Mariotti, a NYC public schoolteacher and president of his own do-it-yourself organization called the National Foundation for Teaching Entrepreneurship. His contribution was to teach the most hopelessly disadvantaged youngsters—kids from the inner city, kids with physical handicaps—how to run their own business. So far he has gotten eighty started—businesses that usually do about $800 in annual sales, though one did $30,000. These are not vast sums, but what happened to the youngsters was wonderful. They learned to take charge of their lives, to link rewards with their own efforts. Their school grades went up, their dropout rate went down, their "aggressive behavior" diminished and their ability to look to the long term improved markedly. The rate of teenage pregnancy among participants went down by a "factor of eight or nine"—one of those astonishing side-effects that no one could have predicted. The girls learned that having a baby to get on welfare is not the only option available to them. "We have found," said Mariotti, "that the primary cause of teenage pregnancy in the inner city is economic ignorance. . . . There is nothing that forces you to look further into the future and set goals for yourself than starting a small business."

Who would expect that the game of chess could be a cure for the street life, drug culture and educational woes of big city schools? The answer is, a lot of individuals who simply love the game, and even some nonprofit programs that will send kids to summer chess camps. Chess is a difficult game that teaches concentration, patience and thinking ahead: surely all pluses for education. Winning is no small personal achievement. Chess is also a game so exciting that it lures youngsters back from street life. It has been a particular boon to black kids from troubled neighborhoods in Harlem and Philadelphia and New York. But there is nothing racial about it at all. I've heard of like results in, for instance, midwestern farm towns. Youngsters who are encouraged to play chess, just like those encouraged to start their own businesses, do better in school and in life.

I could go on and on, but we have space for only a few more cases. Shall we look at the allegedly powerless individual? A Michigan woman got disgusted with racy TV that was "hostile to family values," and raised the roof. She took charge by herself and complained. Others responded to her leadership and soon she could take out full-page ads. Advertisers who supported the too-raunchy shows soon had to run for cover. Africa, as I write, is not sharing the springtime of freedom enjoyed in so much of the world, and remains too hungry as a result. But there are exceptions like Mauritania that listened to some neighborly advice from Americans and adopted free markets. When farmland in Mauritania was switched from communal to private property, rice production went up *twenty-five*fold (!) Wheatley, Idaho; Keller, Texas; Jasper, Alabama and many other small communities are much the richer for getting "collected works of America's foremost authors" from a nonprofit enterprise called "The Library of America." The books distributed are of high quality in both content and binding, but they do not come free. The communities have to pay half, which they have done with good old American bake sales and quilting bees. The Library of America is a big foundation effort, and unfortunately involves some government money (which is our fault, not theirs), but it understands that a joint contribution is the right way to do it. And it does a lot of good, distributing American writings to small towns that could not otherwise afford such fine books. . . . About the last place on earth I would expect educational concern is in a basketball camp run by commercial interests for the best high school players from across the country. I didn't reckon on the Nike/ABCD camp, held each summer at Princeton. The name means Academic Betterment and Career Development, and it's a lot more than a catchphrase. The players are pre-tested in reading, writing and math skills, then get three hours' instruction a day. They are also provided three more hours of daily counseling on drug and alcohol abuse, college rules and how to succeed in class. Of course basketball remains the main focus at the camp, but it's nice that somebody remembers the "college" in college athletics. . . . Lastly, it was a pleasant surprise for me to learn that there are many overtly Christian businesses, and that they do very well in the market. There are at least 7,000 that try to operate according to biblical rules. They face unusual disadvantages, but also find unusual resources. For instance, Chick-fil-A, a fast food concern, both foregoes revenue and is barred from some malls because it won't open on Sundays. But its employees are enthusiastic and committed, and their turnover rate is one-sixth the industry norm. Days Inns, a motel chain, cost itself an estimated 20 percent of net profit by refusing to serve alcohol. But the same policy attracted family trade, and the chain grew to 312 units—and gave away two and a half million Bibles—before being sold. Based on a study of 152 Christian firms, collectively they "grew significantly faster than other companies in their fields by every criterion examined: return on assets, net sales, number of employees and value of net assets."

I'm sorry that there hasn't yet been a follow-up study by some intrigued economist to learn what is different and more successful in these firms. But my own untrained eye can see a few factors. One company reported doing all its business on trust and a handshake; I'll bet its legal costs are rock bottom. The low turnover rate at Chick-fil-A and other firms must reduce job training costs a great deal. More than any specific factor, though, must be the atmosphere of ethical, help-your-neighbor business. Clearly, this is cultivated: almost all the companies conduct on-site religious activities, and most also proselytize customers or even suppliers. Said one businessman, "If you dedicate a business to the good of man, give value and create jobs, you are working for the glory of God." Said another, "God's principles work. If people perceive that they are being treated right, they will break their necks to help you." These are good thoughts for any aspect of our lives, not just business. Yet it is also good to be reminded that business, so often derided by intellectuals and the media, is an ethical as well as creative part of our lives, giving honest value for value received. And here we learn literally *good* business is good business! Walter Lippmann put it even more surprisingly in *The Good Society* more than fifty years ago. The Golden Rule, he said, is economically *efficient*. He was right. *Good* businessmen know it.

There is an old saw that good news is where you find it. I say, good news is where we create it. I don't mean "we, the world." I mean you and I arming ourselves with the right ideas and taking personal responsibility. That is exactly what the creators of these success stories did.

Chapter XIV
TOMORROW'S AGENDA

We need no more than the unrepentant left to remind us that the war of ideas is not over. It may, indeed, grow more intense. The rejection of communism in Eastern Europe leaves a vacuum that other "isms" and ideologies will rush to fill. Certainly among them will be milder forms of socialism and other schemes, such as radical environmentalism, that build the power of the state. It is the business of all of us who stand for individual rights in a civilized order to refute these efforts and make our own ideas heard. The answer to bad ideas is good ideas. Let us never forget that the war of ideas is a real war, with real casualties should we fail.

One cannot predict the politics and perils of tomorrow exactly, but the enemies of the moral order change little. We know them. We can in some measure anticipate their assaults by their beliefs and goals, and plan our own strategy accordingly. The enemy, as ever, will be exploiters, the wielders of power and privilege. They will be the Greens instead of the Reds, the "New Agers," the Satanists, ideologues, tax-takers, utopians, self-serving bureaucrats, the immoral and the irresponsible. They will take positions against the traditional and the normal, against home and family, against distinction between man and woman, against human nature itself: positions which, on analysis, will treat people as mere conveniences to somebody's plans, not as individuals of infinite worth. Whatever they seek, they will be armed with ideological formulas and warped words. Above all, they will try to force their schemes on us all, using the power of government.

Such resort to government "solutions" always seems to me a giveaway that something wrong or dishonest is involved. In freedom, persuasion, not coercion, is the way to get one's idea across, and the only way. Imposing it by law denies to others their liberty, their dignity, their right to their own opinions. It is, in fact, an act of contempt toward them and an act of pride in oneself—a claim to know better than we what is best for us. In the view of Nobel Laureate F. A. von Hayek, this is the "fatal conceit." In the Christian view, it is sin. Deep down, it implies a false, secularist view of life that throughout this century has been at war with American ideals. It is precisely the kind of thinking that has collapsed due to hard experience in Eastern Europe; but it is still rampant here. We need not know the whys and wherefores of a given statist scheme to realize that it serves bent thinking and bad purposes. It will, of course, be made to sound good, as if it were correcting injustice instead of creating it or helping the needy instead of making them dependent and helpless. It will, of course, have the support of all the familiar "opinion makers," joining their voices a cappella. But it is going to cost us dearly, not only in taxes and liberty but in moral values. Consider yourself warned. The red flags are up.

Certainly, in the coming years, we will have to deal with liberalism, a set of once-noble ideas that sold its soul to statism decades ago and now grows more decadent every day. It remains strong, but as a reflex. Tap any liberal knee with a rubber hammer, and any informed person can predict where the leg will jerk. The thrust of it will be an attack on what is normal and morally healthy in favor of things everyone has always regarded as perverse. What else can you say about a view that insists animals have rights and human babies don't? I cannot, offhand, think of anything liberals advocate today that should not be shunned by any honest person. If you'd like to know more about their agenda, tune into PBS for a week and then enter a detoxification program.

Vaguer in its thinking but more dangerous in its effects is an attitude the liberal-left constantly encourages: Uncle Sam should do everything. If we think this, we forget three basic facts of life. First, Sammy can't do anything for us without first taking from us the means to do it. Second, Sammy's only tool is force, and force is usually the worst possible tool to apply in social matters. Police power should be limited to its functions in justice and defense. When we use it to intervene in industry, agriculture, trade or other private functions, we get boondoggles and waste and blundering in epic amounts. Finally, we forget that we ourselves, as free men and women, are the doers and builders and producers. Running to Uncle Sam with every case of sniffles takes away from our own freedom and resources to do and build and produce. We have, I'm afraid, lost our fear of big government, and we had better regain it soon. We seem to see no moral problem with do-everything government, but it is an affront to our rights. We look at the latest trillion-dollar budget and yawn, as if overtaxation were not also morally unsound. America is not immune to suffocation by an Old World-type state, any more than Eastern Europe was. Our survival is at stake until we remember and apply what Jefferson told us: That government is best that governs least. Put this high on the agenda for coming years.

Big government is at its worst in the realms of welfarism and income redistribution. Taking from those who earn to give to those who do not is a formula for destruction. It reduces the value of scarce resources on both sides of the transfer. For the earner, it is a forced salary cut and a disincentive. For the recipient, it is "easy come, easy go" money. The devaluation reduces our national wealth. It is exactly the opposite of free-market exchanges in which both parties gain, increasing wealth. This process is also, we have learned in the last generation, the fast lane to serfdom for those snared in the welfare web.

There is nothing humane about supporting a welfare habit. We are overdue for rethinking our means for assisting those less fortunate. It should start with recognition that the essence of charity is helping people help themselves. Payments based on need instead of on self-help finance permanent failure. Welfare agencies actually measure their success by how much they spend, not by results (try doing that in business!). What we forget in these schemes, really, is that people have a higher nature, that they may appreciate a helping hand but don't want handouts, that they want and need to pay their own way. As Charles Murray noted, people *need* challenge and a sense of competency, and need these things in a deeper, more basic way than they need food and water. They want to carry their own weight. Any welfare program that strips people of their pride and self-responsibility is a rank failure, never mind the cost. The challenge to us is to break the chains of welfare dependency, gently but surely, and to create private instruments to take over. What we should seek are means and incentives for people to better themselves. Jobs and tools are far finer gifts than welfare checks and food stamps. In fact, I see no reason why breaking the welfare cycle should not be an opportunity for entrepreneurs and hence solvable without resorting to charity, in many cases. In any case, if it comes to charity, let it be private and let it be done with that respect and sympathy for the recipient that gives him the freedom to build on his own and that delights in his success.

It is not hard to predict other arenas in the war of ideas in the next few years. Better than looking at them one by one, let's review a few basics that will be tested in every case. For one, every addition to government is a subtraction from liberty, and it will come back to hurt us. It is time to put that process in reverse gear and expand the freedom that is ours by right. We must restore the principle that justice is blind. We have too long suffered the liberals' formula that alleged past private discrimination justifies official and coercive discrimination to compensate, in such programs as Affirmative Action. Two wrongs never make a right. It is wrong for the law ever to favor one citizen over another. Right now we have a slew of "protected classes" under federal law, who comprise a solid majority of the citizenry and who may claim privileged treatment.* Either this scheme goes or America the free goes. They cannot coexist. More than fifty years ago, Walter Lippmann observed, " . . . when modern states abandoned the Jeffersonian principle of special privi-

---

*Another instance of the double devaluation effect of unearned benefits. Those discriminated against lose incentive, those discriminated for find their efforts cheapened and suspect. This has been a prolific breeding ground of resentment and is part of increasing racism on campus and elsewhere. The effect shows up also in lowered university admission standards and preferential grading for minorities, making their work that much more suspect.

leges to none they become committed to the principle of special privileges for all." Special privileges for all is a ghastly idea. Special privileges for some at the expense of others is worse. The only answer fair to all is to work our way back to Jefferson and give up on the "modern" state. Incidentally, this would save us perhaps a trillion dollars a year, or $4,000 a person. Could your family use the extra income? Which brings us roundabout to the last and most fundamental point of all, that all this do-goodery and privilege is financed by taxation. Taxes, to put it gently—we will leave it to Mark Twain, Will Rogers and Fred Allen to note any similarities to armed robbery—are an involuntary exaction from the private, productive economy: which happens to be all we have to live on. The more the government takes, the less we are allowed for private consumption and investment. (Five of the six richest counties in America are clustered around Washington, D.C.—bedroom communities of the government.) We have gone from the least-taxed nation on earth, back when the American Revolution was in fashion and on into this century, to the nation with the highest tax toll in all known history. This, too, must be reversed.

Earlier I noted that taxes are a disincentive to production. What we tax, we get less of, just as we get more of what we subsidize. These are economic laws, not political theories. If our social objective is to erase poverty, we should be taxing it, not paying for it. If our objective is to become wealthier, we should encourage production, not tax it. Taxing the "ability to pay" (otherwise known as "soak the rich") is in fact taxing our ability to invest and produce. Don't get me wrong, I don't advocate coddling the rich or oppressing the poor with tax laws. I am just pointing out that we are doing things exactly wrong now and are getting all the hunger and inequality we tax and pay for. But much the greater problem is the taxes themselves. We pay vastly too much in taxes and it is creating chaos. All we do in tolerating this is feed an overweening government and steal the lives of our own children, who will have to pay for it. Already an irresponsible Congress spends more every year than it can tax, piling up debts it expects our children to pay. History tells us this is national suicide. There is only one way to stop it and that is cutting off the stream of excess taxes. Mr. Jefferson approved. A little rebellion now and then is a good thing, he said.

Final Thoughts

> To the masses of the western world the news that all men are more than things was proclaimed by the Christian gospel and was celebrated in its central mysteries. It proclaimed the news to all men that they were not brute things, to all men without exception, the weak, the outcast, the downtrodden, the enslaved, and the utterly dejected. The influence of that gospel has been inexhaustible. It anchored the rights of men in the structure of the universe. It set these rights apart where they were beyond human interference. Thus the pretensions of despots became heretical. And since that revelation, though many despots have had the blessings of the clergy, no tyranny has possessed a clear title before the tribunal of human conscience, no slave has had to feel that the hope of freedom was forever foreclosed. For in the recognition that there is in each man a final essence—that is to say, an immortal soul—which only God can judge, a limit was set upon the dominion of men over men. The prerogatives of supremacy were radically undermined. The inviolability of the human person was declared.
> —Walter Lippmann (*The Good Society*)

We see momentous change around us, but cannot be sure where it will take us. Will a springtime of liberty bloom into a full summer of peace? Or will our hopes collapse before some new peril? Surely it is up to us to create the right tomorrow for our children by taking charge today.

There has never been a generation in the history of America which has had such an enormous opportunity to make a clear choice and to have a hand in implementing that choice. We can play our part in shaping the world now emerging, or we can stand aside and be overrun. The other side is working against us. We have to be better. We have to lead with the right ideas.

When we cut through all the economic and political cant, we recognize that the real problem before us is lack of leadership. We don't have nearly enough leaders. The moral qualities that make us leaders have been eroded by long years of false thinking. When somebody tries to lead, the first instinct of the herd is to tear him down. We have moved a long way from the idea of the hero. We have allowed anti-heroes to befoul our morals, manners and culture. Only a willingness to face them down and say that right is right can restore the health of the Republic.

I submit that you and I have the obligation to lead and that we cannot delegate it to anyone else. We simply cannot turn over to others our integrity, our conscience or our religious beliefs.

Meeting our obligation of leadership requires us to realize that ideas, not armies, rule the world. This lesson was brought home to me once again as I finished this book. I have an almost eerie sense that the book could not have been finished before it was. If it had been done sooner, as I intended, it would have missed some of the signal events of modern times. A book, every author learns, takes on a life of its own, and "A writer grimly controls his work to his peril," writes Madeleine L'Engle. She adds, "Slowly, slowly I am learning to listen to the book, in the same way I listen to prayer." May we, too, listen as to prayer; for I believe that the book is telling us that we should have had more faith in what we know is true. Ideas, not armies, rule the world. We believed too easily that the tanks and barbed wire and secret police and instruments of thought control of totalitarian power were decisive, and that slaves could never be free. The events in Eastern Europe proved us wrong. It was false belief, not barbed wire, that enslaved. In the end, the wire was cut and the Berlin Wall broken by simple human choice, not arms. Those who had been trapped behind the barricades said, "Enough!" and were free. The lesson must not be lost again.

Our obligation to lead equally requires us to accept individual responsibility; to strengthen the moral and spiritual foundations of conduct; and to learn history's lessons and apply them. All of these are necessary to arm us for the battle of ideas before us.

I have suggested above some of the directions this battle may lead. In a deeper sense, it all comes back to one struggle: to restore a sound spiritual foundation to our own lives and to our national life. Our political, economic and social problems have a common moral and spiritual root. They spring from long indulgence of a materialistic view of life. According to this view, we have no responsibility to God so there are no real moral restraints on our conduct. This leads to the worst philosophy of all: "anything goes." Can we be surprised that we are flooded with cultural filth, promiscuity, tax addicts, venereal disease, foul language, crime, pornography and selfishness?

This kind of thinking is the ultimate irresponsibility. It denies any obligation to others, much less to God. It breaks the bonds of human sympathy. It even stoops to exploiting others, clamoring for benefits from "the government" that really come off someone else's table. The state feasts on personal selfishness.

We see again that statism rages where religious belief wanes. The *Federalist Papers* predicted that we would lose our liberty if we did not remain virtuous. Tocqueville said we were a nation "with the soul of a church"; would anyone say this is still true? It is certainly not the soul of a church that prompts some among us to dip a figurine of Christ in urine and call it art, or to record screeches of praise to the Devil and call it music.

We must recover the plain truth that all civilization is based on shared religious belief: that is, a common understanding about what is right and what is wrong. On this alone are sound institutions built. It is persons of integrity who must build them, recognizing that we are all children of God and responsible to God, to ourselves and to one another. Only by acknowledging a divine basis for life can we guarantee the inalienable rights of the person against the never-ending predations of the state. We answer to a Higher Power; the state therefore may not have final control over our lives, nor deny us the freedom to exercise our responsibility to God. For two thousand years, these ideas have proven themselves, as the foundation of the West and the bulwark of our liberty. All Americans believed them once, but our values have been undermined, and our certainty in them shaken.

For a hundred years, the same foundations have been under mean and ceaseless attack from secular ideology. We have found out to our sorrow where this is taking us. But it isn't systems or laws or alleged patterns of history that determine our fate, as our detractors say. What shapes the world is what we make of ourselves, one by one. Blaming others for our shortcomings is simply childish. Ideology raises such childishness to a fine art, blaming capitalists or Jews or some other hated THEM for social troubles. Any adult ought to know better. And we had better realize that shirking our responsibilities will not only get things fouled up as usual but make the baby-talk philosophers look prophetic. But that doesn't make their case less childish. The only way we will ever have a good society is by making good people of ourselves, who *are* society.

To function as leaders, then, we have to appeal to goodness and build on moral premises. We have to offer solutions based on our spiritual understanding. It has been my unfailing experience that when you exercise leadership from these premises, you attract a following of right-thinking people immediately. Many among us hunger for the traditional American understandings and a moral regeneration. You hardly have to look for them. Speak to them in the language of goodness and they will come looking for you. Put before them the challenge of self-transcendence, the ability to better ourselves that sets us apart from beasts in the field: they will welcome their responsibility.

On these terms, the list of potential leaders is a long one. All of us can be and indeed are leaders in our own way in various walks of life. Hillsdale College has acted on this principle for many years. You may call us old fashioned, but we believe our duty to our students is to develop their individuality and leadership to the fullest—not to stamp out identical group-thinking units. We delight in their diversity, and we work hard to help each bring out the best within him, one by one. We have guarded our independence precisely in order that we may carry out this duty. It works. I see it work every day as our students gain the capabilities, confidence and adult sense of responsibility of future leaders. Our outreach programs—the Shavano Institute, the Center for Constructive Alternatives, *Imprimis*—are based on the same understanding, and the response has been wonderful. All around the country people gather with us and help build a leadership community that can restore America. I am here to tell you that the same can be done by any of us. The same *is* done every day by neighbors, friends, teachers, clergymen and others in every community. All take a role whose thoughts are clear and whose heart is good.

The challenge before us is to start a revolution in moral understanding. I do not speak idly. The challenge has never been tougher. But the time has never been more right, nor the opportunity greater. Back in what we think of as the tame and normal 1950s, one man saw more clearly than we that we were at a turning point. He is one of my favorite mentors, Canon Bernard Iddings Bell, and he issued the same challenge: "Our present difficulties are so great and so basic as to demand nothing short of revolution; not so much political revolution or economic revolution as moral revolution—a revolution in estimate and pursuit of values." No one heeded. The turning came. In the years that followed, a decadent liberalism turned nihilist and spread an evil rot through the foundations of American idealism. All of us of an age remember it, remember the feeling that the times had gone mad, that our sense of purpose and belonging was gone, that no one knew what it was to be an American any more.

Another turning has come. This time we must heed the clear warning and lead the moral revolution. I do not even want to think what will become of us if we fail this time. No one else will do it for us. Our task is more difficult because the rot is still with us: it urinates on our most holy symbols. But the opportunity that has come is a turning back to the real America. We are not called on to save the world. That has been done for us. We are asked only to put our hearts and souls right, for in this all else shall be added. You and I can and must be part of it.

Let us rejoice in the chance. We Americans specialize in liberty. Let freedom ring! Where the Spirit of the Lord is, said the prophet, there is liberty. In that Spirit, we will reclaim our own and cannot be denied.

EPILOGUE

My burden in this book has been to uphold our moral nature, our innate freedom and a human scale of life for each of us. We are, one and all, unique individuals on this earth, joined by a common humanity and a sense of transcendent purpose. We are not ants in an anthill. Our daily struggles to rise above ourselves have meaning beyond time. Every life is precious. This is an old-fashioned view of the human condition, but it has passed the test of experience for thirty centuries or more.

In modern times, our traditional understandings have come under genocidal attack from theorists of the anthill. There have been no end of "group-think" theories saying that the collective is the only thing, and that we cannot be happy until we radically change ourselves to be a part of the group. Our race, our class, our sex, our religion, our society: that is what matters, they say; you and I are nothing. Individuals are nothing. This new view flies in the face of traditional wisdom, and in fairness, it should have the burden of proof. It has been tested to death (all too literally in much of the world) and should be able to say to us, this is what works. Its defenders should have better arguments than comparing their utopian dreams with the everyday and not so pleasant realities we all deal with. But they do not. Group-think fails everywhere it is tried. It does not understand the human life or its place in the cosmos. Most of all it fails to see us as children of God. All the modern "isms" share the view that God is nothing and Man, in some collective form, is the center of being. The result of this idea is always and inevitably the glorification of the state and the subjugation of people born free. But we were never intended to be slaves.

I have tried to accept in this book what the utopians cannot: the burden of proof. Words and arguments are fine, but hard facts and figures speak louder. I cannot, of course, cite all the facts that damn the collectivist theories—they would fill a large library. But I have tried to touch on some that are important and that we can all easily understand. And I have tried to do so (if you will excuse these last few paragraphs) with a commodity that the "utopias" could never offer: a genuinely human smile.

You and I know, and maybe all the world will know one day, that when our lives are given salvation and eternal hope, every day can be exciting and joyous and fun instead of bleak and grim. When we remember the old teachings and understand them, happiness is given to us freely. Of old, the angels told us, "Rejoice and be exceedingly glad. . . . "

New-think gave us barbed wire, machine guns, slavery and life stripped of meaning by the Second Law of Thermodynamics. Everybody hated it. Many died trying to escape it and many more found God in the teeth of (or because of) its slave labor camps and engines of thought control. What more do we need to know about it?

I love to laugh, and I'll bet you do too. We *can* laugh and we do, simply by accepting life as a gift from the God who called His creation good. The words, "Thy will be done," give our lives just the right foundation. Without them, we build our houses on sand and will never find a real smile. With them we are the salt of the earth, and we do, one by one, each with his own gifts, all that is good in this world.

If we are called on to do even more than we do now, it is not a burden but a blessing.

INDEX

George Roche, noted historian and educator, is the president of Hillsdale College in Michigan, a school esteemed for its academic excellence, liberal arts emphasis, and independence. Formerly the presidentially appointed chairman of the National Council on Educational Research, he is the author of seven books on education, history, philosophy and government, including *A World Without Heroes: The Modern Tragedy*, *America by the Throat: The Stranglehold of Federal Bureaucracy*, and two works of fiction, *Going Home* and *A Reason for Living*.

For more information on books offered by the Hillsdale College Press or on Hillsdale College and its fight to remain independent of federal funds and federal control, please contact: Hillsdale College Press, Hillsdale, Michigan 49242; 800/535-0860.